INCURABLY ROMANTIC

INCURABLY ROMANTIC

BERNARD F. STEHLE

Afterword by
Joseph W. Schneider

*For Linda — Who understands
the basic truths,*

F. Stehle

10 Nov. 1992

Temple University Press ▪ Philadelphia

Temple University Press, Philadelphia 19122
© 1985 by Bernard F. Stehle. All rights reserved
Published 1985
Printed in the United States of America

Library of Congress Cataloging in Publication Data

Stehle, Bernard F.
    Incurably romantic.

    1. Physically handicapped—United States—Biography.
2. Physically handicapped—United States—Biography—
Pictorial works.   3. Love.   4. Love—Pictorial works.
I. Title.
HV3012.S83   1985   362.4′3′0922   [B]   84-8727
ISBN 0-87722-307-6

*To my Mother and Father—and to those
residents of Inglis House who did not live to
see it published—I dedicate this work*

"What we call basic truths are simply the ones
we discover after all the others."

Albert Camus, *The Fall*

ACKNOWLEDGMENTS

While it is impossible to thank everyone who has contributed so much to this book during the past four years, I do wish to name a few, at least, and have them stand for all.

I express my deepest thanks to all the residents of Inglis House who shared so much of their lives with me; my own life has been immeasurably enriched as a result—and will undoubtedly continue to be. I am also thankful for their kind cooperation to Frank Gable, President of Inglis House; Carol Purdie, Director of Social Service; Paula and Mark Silver, Educational Coordinators (and the most dedicated teachers I have ever known); and Mrs. Clifton F. West, Jr., Chairman of the Board of Directors.

At Community College of Philadelphia, I am indebted especially to Alison Tasch, former Chairman of the English Department, and to Tom Ott, present Chairman. Their styles of leadership have fostered openness and a spirit of collegiality within the department, allowing students and faculty to develop themselves and their ideas as fully and creatively as possible. Similar appreciation extends to Allan Kobernick, Chairman of the Photography Department, for his dedication to excellence and supportive attitude and cooperation in helping others achieve the products of their vision. Many other colleagues looked, listened, and offered valuable critical comments throughout the project, especially Paul McGarvey, Luke Russell, Richie Clark, William C. Thompson, Joseph Hanley, Terri Oliver, Don Weinberg and C. Geoffrey Berken. Their friendship and professional talents continue to be a source of special pride and inspiration.

For their encouragement and advice early on in the work, I am grateful to several friends and former colleagues at Horizon House, Inc., namely, Tom O'Hara, Marvin Elias, Robert Kay, Deborah Kulp, Joel Esterman, Fran Caporale, and Britton Jones. For their critical insights offered at different stages of the work, I thank Michael Hausman, filmhaus, inc., New York; the late Lee Witkin, the

Witkin Gallery, New York; Eileen Kaye Berger, International Center of Photography, New York; Steve Williams, formerly of The Photography Place, Philadelphia; Mrs. Ginny Thornburgh, First Lady of Pennsylvania; Peggy Capps, Drew CMHC, Philadelphia; Joseph R. Foley, Philadelphia; Richard and Kathleen Serano and Marge Russell, also of Philadelphia.

I would never have made it through certain weeks and months without the generous material support of Lorraine Cahn, Ed Stehle, Nora Levin, James H. Allen, Judith Stehle, James Crowley, and Mary Jo Crowley. To them, and to my parents as well, I voice my appreciation for making it possible to keep going just when it seemed, again and again, truly impossible.

For their sensitive reading and suggestions late in the project, I am grateful to Emily Chernikoff, Meg Givnish, Susan Romberger, and Marian Garfinkel. Also in these later stages I am thankful to William and Theresa West and Agnes Cedrone for helping me meet various deadlines. Finally, I wish to acknowledge the Pennsylvania Council on the Arts for the 1984 Fellowship in the Visual Arts they awarded me in order to complete the last phase of the book.

Finally, I thank David Bartlett, Director of Temple University Press, for his frequent wise counsel and commitment to the vision of this work; his enthusiasm never flagged from the moment he saw the first photographs in April 1983. And to Michael Ames, Editor-in-Chief, I give my special thanks for sparing no effort again and again in achieving creative as well as practical solutions to the seemingly endless details and complexities peculiar to a work of this sort.

CONTENTS

INTRODUCTION

This book of portraits is about love relationships where one or both of the couple is severely physically disabled. The inspiration for it occurred during a teaching assignment for Community College of Philadelphia. In January, 1980, I was asked by a colleague in the English Department if I would be interested in teaching a composition course at Inglis House, known then as The Philadelphia Home for Incurables.

All twelve students in my class were in wheelchairs. Like the other nearly four hundred residents, they had problems such as cerebral palsy, muscular dystrophy, multiple sclerosis, quadriplegia—these and other illnesses and conditions, some of which, like friedreich's ataxia, I had never heard of before—and some had multiple disabilities.

In the third or fourth class of the fall 1980 term, we were discussing the importance of sincerity in writing—as important to forming effective sentences and paragraphs, I was suggesting, as it is to forming good relationships. In pursuing this analogy, we soon found ourselves engrossed in exchanging personal stories and ideas about the nature of love, about our concepts of freedom, commitment, dependency and independence, and about marriage, fidelity, communication problems, and so forth. I had not suspected there would be so many people in the class capable of contributing to such a discussion; but there were, and all had their own accounts of being in and out of love. One woman with cerebral palsy, for example, told us of the informal ceremony in Founder's Hall she and her boyfriend had arranged in 1979; they had vowed forever their love and friendship and exchanged rings before a circle of their most intimate friends. Another woman, paralyzed from the chest down, told how much she loved her boyfriend but was continuing to see other men as well because she didn't want, in her words, "to be tied down to one relationship." A man so severely crippled that he could not sit up at all and could speak only with the greatest effort, spoke of the difficulty of being in a long-distance relationship with his blind girlfriend who lived in Virginia. It went on like this for an hour or so until, struck by the number of "incurables" before me who were so openly sharing their wide range of feelings and experiences as lovers (so much in contrast to the negative assumptions induced by that forbidding sign in front of the building), I blurted out: "So *that's* why they call this place the Home for *Incurables*—you're incurably *romantic*!"

Over the next three years I talked to more residents of Inglis House about their relationships, bringing my cameras and tape recorder along for the book everyone soon came to know I was making. The text and photographs which resulted represent an unusual collaborative effort. For instance, whenever I was asked where I wanted to take the photographs, I responded by asking the couple to choose their own intimate space—the place *they* defined as special in some way or where they simply enjoyed spending time together. Many couples never left the room in which we had begun the conversation, but others exercised quite a variety of choices. One resident, a widower, wanted a portrait made in the lobby in front of the stained glass mirror his son had made and donated to Inglis House. Another resident, four months pregnant at the time, wanted her photograph taken in front of the huge Christmas tree in Founder's Hall. In another instance, one couple and I had planned on making some photographs in her room the day she was leaving for a brief Easter vacation with her family. As it turned out, neither of them was in her room at the appointed time, but later I ran into them in the basement laundry room; we ended up talking at some length about their relationship—and making the pictures there.

Intimate space was sometimes very public. One couple chose to be photographed in front of the sliding-glass doors just outside the building's main entrance. In contrast, another couple, very protective of their privacy, chose to have me photograph their intimate space—but without them in it. "This is like our shrine," she said of her room, "the place where we spend our best times together."

Two other choices of location may serve to further suggest how unpredictable and revelatory such collaboration could prove to be. Despite my initial incredulity, one resident—a poet—insisted that he really did want a portrait composed in front of the electrical power station, behind the main building. With whom? With the only "lover" he had at that time ("but a faithful one," he added)—his typewriter! So we did it; he orchestrating the whole thing down to the last witty detail—the electrical cord plugged into the palm of his left hand.

Another resident, a woman who had decided to separate from her husband and to move out of Inglis House into an apartment of her own, led me out the front door of the building one afternoon and along the curved driveway toward the oak tree she had told me about a few days earlier. Swelling with a sense of freedom and independence she said she hadn't felt for a long time, she balked at my concern about getting her chair over the curb and—to my complete surprise—rose up out of her wheelchair, waved my uncertain hands away, and somehow balanced herself enough to walk to the tree on her own power. I made some photographs of her standing there. She had chosen to wear the same dress she had worn on the day of her wedding.

Once they had chosen a location, couples usually expected me to pose them, but instead I would ask them to be together in whatever way they liked. One way one woman expresses love for her boyfriend, who cannot use his hands to feed himself, just as she cannot, is by feeding him using a fork held between her teeth, as she chose to do for one of the photographs. In another instance, a couple I was photographing spent the entire hour and a half arguing their usual topic: whether in fact she was using her disability as an excuse for not doing more of what he felt she was capable of, both within and outside their relationship. They never got closer than six feet to each other. Other couples sometimes held hands, even some I had never imagined could do so, for early on I had wondered: Did people who couldn't hold a pencil in their hands, hold hands? Did it *matter* whether they could or not? What *did* matter?

In making photographs I attempted neither to deny people's obvious physical handicaps nor to emphasize them. Such disabilities are part of what is given about their presence, so they are often part of what is present in the photographs. And instead of suppressing the questions and fears their physical conditions sometimes evoked in me, I voiced them. This often became the very way into our discussing all the other, more important things about them—which then affected our photographic sessions. For the more they came to trust my interest in them as persons, the more they seemed to trust their own body-image before the camera. Acceptance was a mutual need—and some obstacles mutual as well, in their own way. Just as it mattered to them that I see beyond their wheelchairs, for example, it mattered to me that they see beyond my cameras and tripod. In order to begin to feel understood, we each had our alienating, everpresent mechanical devices we needed the other to be finally forgetful of.

All photographs of a couple were not always made on the same day; sometimes weeks, months, even a year or more might elapse between sessions. Sometimes it was the importance of a change in appearance that occasioned additional photographs. I made pictures of one couple out on the grounds in the Fall of 1980, for example, then met with them again in the Spring, in his room, for some more. She wanted a picture showing off her new front teeth, and he wanted one showing off her legs.

What I have tried to reflect in these photographic statements and verbal snapshots is something of how the people themselves, in so many different ways, see themselves. I took a number of photographs using different lenses, and from angles that I, for the most part, chose. And that obviously is significant. What is also significant is that the couples structured the greater part of the experience themselves.

I printed a number of photographs and showed them to each of the couples, requesting their approval for certain images to be used in the book. All the photographs, and all the text selected from conversations and tapes, have the approval of the residents and non-residents represented in the book. Some people with whom I discussed my work chose not to be photographed at all or, once photographed, in a few cases, opted not to be included in the project.

The reader should understand that in the course of taking photographs over a period of several years, serendipitous things happen and sometimes make for unplanned ironies. The picture of the glass ballerina, for example, was taken when the couple asked me to remove the newly repaired figurine from the box it had just been returned in, and to place it inside the glass bell jar they had been keeping it in before its left leg, bent back at the knee, had broken off. As a little girl, the woman had dreamed of becoming a ballerina (her mother's dream for her as well, she added) and had taken ballet lessons—until her left leg had become so bent backwards as a result of a disease called distonia musculorum deformis that she could no longer even walk. On another occasion, I was photographing a couple—a Black woman and a Jewish man, both severely disabled with cerebral palsy—in his room while he was typing something and she was watching a special on TV. An ironic circumstance, recorded in one of the photographs, is the appearance on the screen of the figure of Hitler standing bolt upright, arms crossed, facing out from the TV in a posture of contempt.

By definition, this book focuses on couples who were couples at the time the book was put together. It includes couples where both partners are residents of Inglis House and couples where only one person is institutionalized. With the passage of time, there have been changes in many of the relationships—break-ups, marriages, separations, divorces, new romances, deaths—some of which show up in the pages that follow.

In the background is another issue. The very crisis of one partner's having to enter an institution challenges couples like nothing else, precipitating the demise of some relationships, deepening others. "As soon as I heard the sound of my neck breaking," one woman told me of her accident in 1981, "I knew our marriage was over." She hasn't seen her husband since she entered Inglis House.

Another woman reports that her husband says, "Too much trouble," when she asks him to take her home for the day. "You know, sometimes I call my number," the same woman says, "and a *woman* answers the phone, and one time I said, 'What are *you* doing in the house?' She says, 'I *live* here.' I said, 'Since *when*?' She says, 'I've lived here for years.' I said, '*Really*?' I probably got a wrong number, but it preys on my mind."

In contrast, a man told me of his reaction when he and his wife discovered in 1947 that she had multiple sclerosis: "We were determined to fight this thing that was fighting us." In 1983, thirty-six years of setbacks and uncertainties later, the two of them were telling me one day in December how no less determined they still are.

And no less in love, either, they further confided (but in separate conversations, for they never spoke so romantically of each other in the other's presence). The only thing they seemed less than sure of that day, in fact, was whether she would be well enough in two weeks' time to make the trip to New Jersey for the party their children were giving them for their fiftieth wedding anniversary.

Philadelphia, February 1984

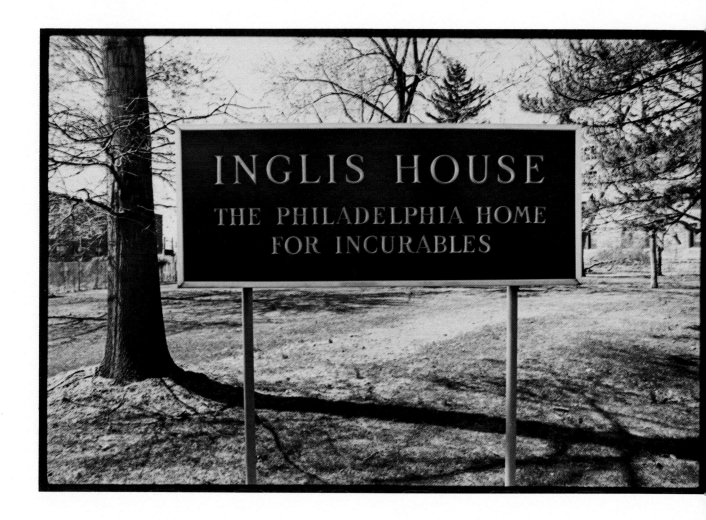

ONE

BOB and JANE

DANNY and DONNA

LOIS and ANDY

BOB AND JANE

JANE

There was a time when I couldn't reach him . . . Now he's more patient, loving, understanding. . . . I think it was Lennon's death that brought us even closer together. We heard one of the cuts—"Starting Over"—and I said, 'Honey, I know you don't like the Beatles, but I want you to listen to this song.' At the end, Bob said to me 'Why can't we start over, put aside our differences?' And I said, O.K., but I can't do it all.' . . . Now we're working it out together.

BOB

I want to take her out some evening to a nice dance floor. I know we can't dance, but I want to take her somewhere where I can be alone with her and have some soft music playing in the background. . . .

DANNY AND DONNA

DONNA

Whenever I leave him I always say: 'Dan, I *love* you.' I could be just going up to the ladies' room here; I'd say 'Dan, I love you.' He'd say: 'I love you too, Buttons.' He always calls me 'Buttons.' I guess [she smiles] because I can't handle buttons. . . .

DANNY:

My father told me before he died, he said: 'Boy, if you find a woman, you stick with her through thick and thin' . . . 'And [Donna, interrupting] he does.'

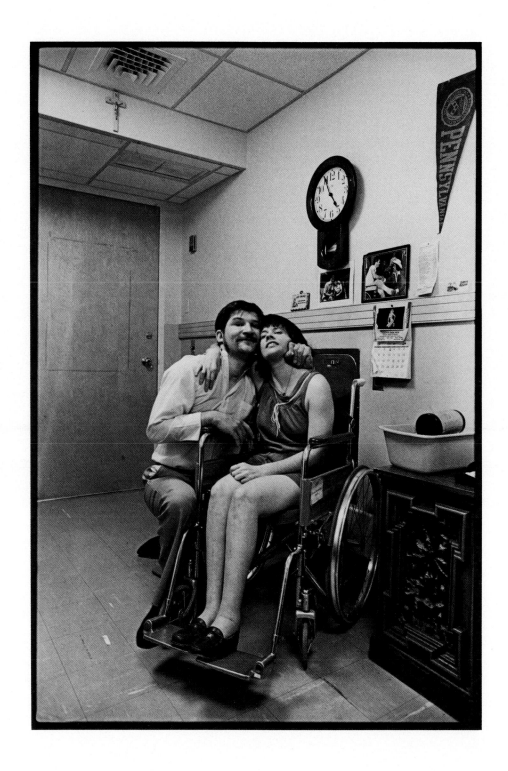

DANNY AND DONNA

ANDY

We first met each other about five years ago [at a cerebral palsy center] . . . but we sure weren't like this. When she saw me when we picked her up in the van, a girl said: 'Here, Lo, here's a guy for you! [but] she didn't want no parts of me, and I guess I didn't want no parts of her; but *now* look at us. . . .

LOIS

We like just being with each other. . . . I feel like I can talk to him about anything.

LOIS AND ANDY

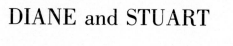

DIANE and STUART

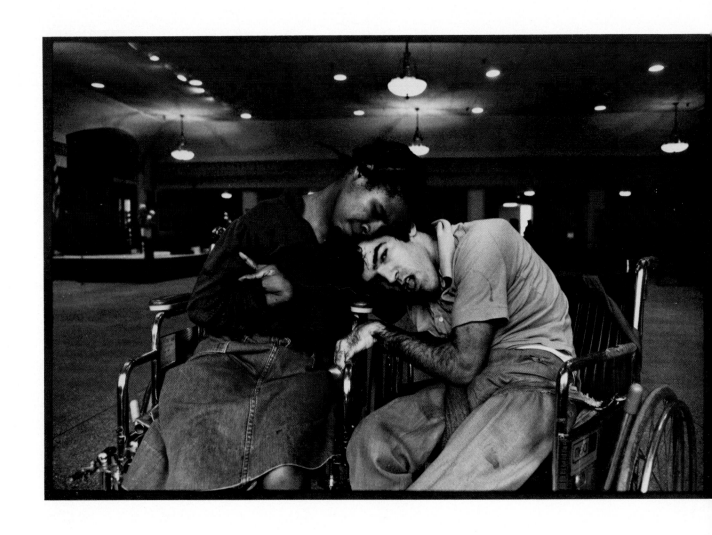

STUART

Diane is the first woman who realized that I had normal feelings of love and of being in love. She makes me happy just holding me and being there. Five years together have taught us a great deal about ourselves. . . . It's a wonderful feeling having someone I can go to for understanding my crazy moods.

DIANE

I said it wouldn't work. But his stubbornness made it work—not to give up on me because of our different backgrounds. Now we are working on it together . . . we are talking.

DIANE AND STUART

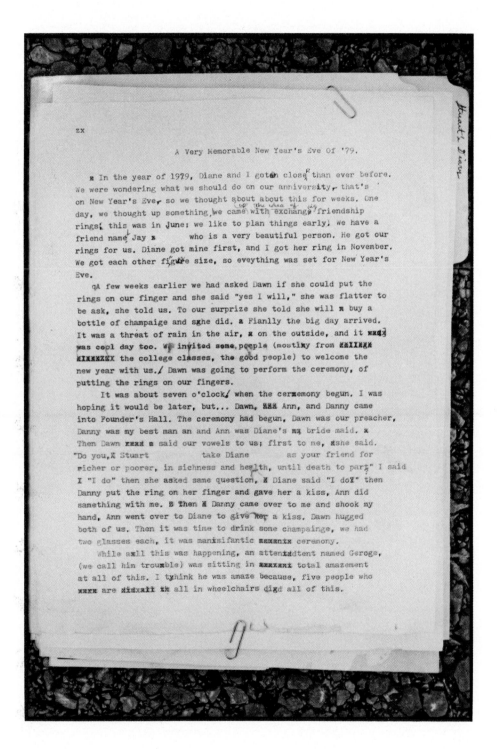

zx

Stuart Diary

A Very Memorable New Year's Eve Of '79.

In the year of 1979, Diane and I goten closer than ever before.
We were wondering what we should do on our anniversity, that's
on New Year's Eve, so we thought about about this for weeks. One
day, we thought up something, we came with exchange friendship
rings, this was in June; we like to plan things early, we have a
friend name Jay x   who is a very beautiful person. He got our
rings for us. Diane got mine first, and I got her ring in November.
We got each other figure size, so eveything was set for New Year's
Eve.

qA few weeks earlier we had asked Dawn if she could put the
rings on our finger and she said "yes I will," she was flatter to
be ask, she told us. To our surprize she told she will x buy a
bottle of champaige and sxhe did. a Fianlly the big day arrived.
It was a threat of rain in the air, x on the outside, and it xxdy
was cool day too. We invited some people (mostlxy from xxIIxxx
xIxxxxXxX the college classes, the good people) to welcome the
new year with us. Dawn was going to perform the ceremony, of
putting the rings on our fingers.

It was about seven o'clock when the cermemony begun. I was
hoping it would be later, but... Dawn, xxx Ann, and Danny came
into Pounder's Hall. The ceremony had begun, Dawn was our preacher,
Danny was my best man an and Ann was Diane's nx bride maid. x
Then Dawn xxxx n said our vowels to us; first to me, xshe said.
"Do you, x Stuart   take Diane   as your friend for
richer or poorer, in sichness and health, until death to part" I said
x "I do" then she asked same question, x Diane said "I dox" then
Danny put the ring on her finger and gave her a kiss, Ann did
samething with me. Ø Then x Danny came over to me and shook my
hand, Ann went over to Diane to give her a kiss. Dawn hugged
both of us. Then it was time to drink some champainge, we had
two glasses each, it was manxsifantic xxxxnxx ceremony.

While axll this was happening, an attenxxdtent named Geroge,
(we call him trouxble) was sitting in xxxxxxx total amazement
at all of this. I txhink he was amaze because, five people who
xxxx are xidxxxx xh all in wheelchairs dixd all of this.

DIANE AND STUART

PEGGY and JIM

BUDDY and GINA

VIKI and ROLAND

JIM

To Peggy

Every day when I awake
And you're not there beside me
I feel very much alone
I feel like I'm a desert
That nobody wants to cross
Every day when I awake
And you're not there beside me.

PEGGY

What keeps us together? I think maybe when we're apart, you know, when we go our own way—kind of leave a space in between, a little time to be away—and when we come together we're glad to see each other. . . . If we didn't give each other space, then what would bring us together? Nothing.

BUDDY

I love her figure, her beautiful hair, and her heart.

GINA

Love most about him? His sweetness, his smiling, his happy-go-lucky kind of way. . . .

VIKI AND ROLAND

ROLAND

[What would you like to see happen in the relationship?] Get married, I guess. Have a lot of children, and all that goes with it. And all that makes that happen. Nice comfortable home. She should stay home while I go out and earn a living for us. I guess that's about it. Drive a car, my own car—and it doesn't have to be a snazzy one either. One that's dependable. One that gets you and brings you. How's that one? That, too, is about it. That's the dream on my part. I don't know what *she's* dreaming about. . . .

VIKI

I thought I was just friends with him, but he's—I found it out that day you were interviewing us—that he loves me [sighs, worriedly]. I just want to be friends with him. . . . I've got to get over the—over him being too lovey-dovey, if you know what I mean. . . . Anyway, I said, 'We can only be friends, or else the relationship will have to end.' . . .

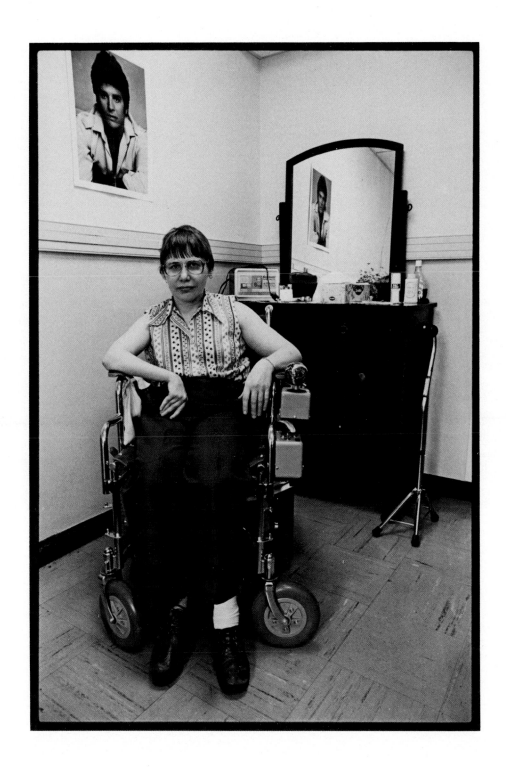

TWO

FLORENCE and JACK

MARYANNE

MARGARET and HENRY

GAIL and GREGORY

ANNE

FRANK

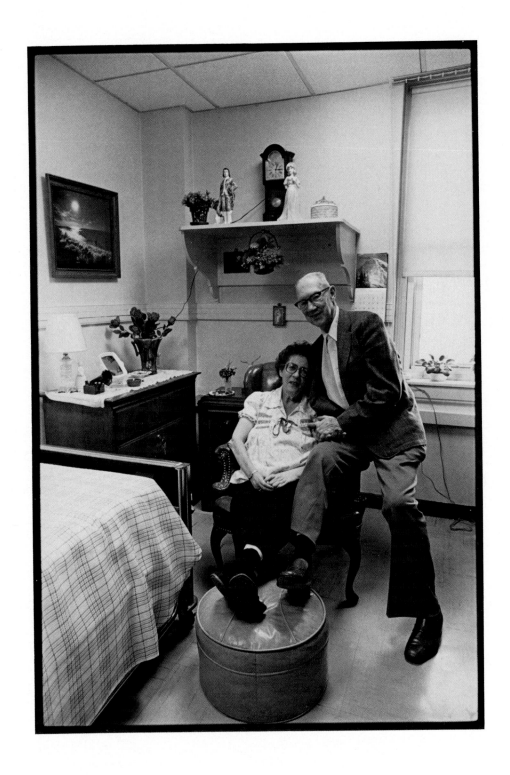

FLORENCE AND JACK

JACK

I was a radio and television repairman and I was called to their home [Florence and her mother's] about twenty-five years ago to repair their TV set. And I'd been coming to their house where they've moved at different places and times ever since, and eventually I got to know her fairly well. Used to take her out occasionally—shopping, mostly, at first; then, when she moved here [1978], I used to take her out to restaurants and various places of interest—take a ride once in awhile to the Poconos, or down the shore. We both are born-again Christians. . . .

I was married *twice*. My first was a divorce; the second one, my wife a couple years ago passed away. So that's the reason we didn't get together—because I was already *married*. And then when she passed away, then once—when I came here one time to fix the set, she said she very seldom gets out—maybe twice a year or so; so I said, 'Well, I have more time now, I'll be glad to take you out occasionally.' So I took her out . . . and to my home, and had meals there and discussed various aspects of the Bible and things like that.

FLORENCE

He *knows* me. . . . I've never met anyone just exactly like him, and I think he's unique. . . . He has a good *mind*—he likes to think things through. If I do something that he doesn't seem [to think is] just the way that I *should* do it, he'll tell me, and I *like* that because you have to be honest in your feelings. . . . He'll do anything in his power to do if I need something. A nice person, I would say. . . .

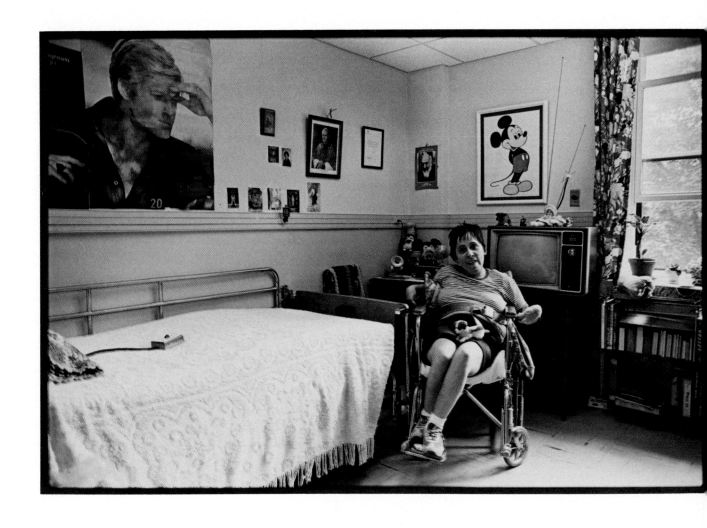

MARYANNE

I didn't know he was going *for good* [when her boyfriend went home for the Christmas holidays, 1981]. I presume *he* knew, but he didn't want to hurt me. I saw him before I went home [for the holidays]. I said, 'Good-bye . . . hope I see you when I come back.' He didn't answer me. He just said, 'We'll see.' From that, I knew he wasn't gonna come back. . . .

I never knew a more kind, gentle, warm-hearted person. Maybe our relationship would have grown. . . . At the same time, life must go on—no matter how hurt you feel, no matter how rejected you feel sometimes. And that's what I try to do—I try to go on . . .

MARGARET AND HENRY

MARGARET

We need somebody, so I have Henry. And he is good to me.

HENRY

She's been married twice already. . . . All I want to do is just put my arm around her. . . . I call her 'Dolly.' . . .

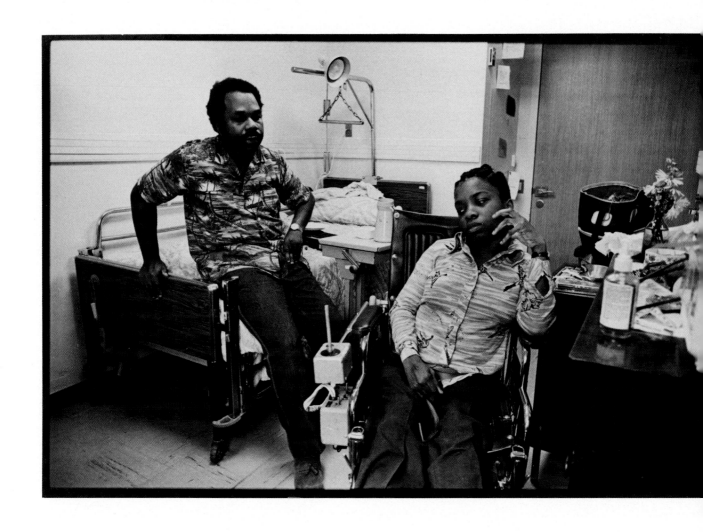

GAIL AND GREGORY

GREGORY

We're so much alike. Up until I was twenty-four years old [he's thirty-one now] I was just like Gail: stubborn, couldn't tell me anything, mean, didn't want to listen, mumble, walkin' around with my mouth stuck out—sound familiar? Blaming everyone else for my problems, not recognizing I was the cause of all my problems, saying 'One day'—not realizing that as long as you say 'One day' you'll never do anything—as long as you never commit yourself, and you'll be in that position *fifty years* from now, hopin' for 'One day'; lazy, wanted my way all the time, didn't care about anyone else, out for what I can get. Then I felt sex was the answer to everything—thought that would solve everything, wanted every woman that I could get. . . .

I thought the world owed me something when I was twenty-four years old, and if I didn't get my way— I tell her [Gail] she's like a 'little Gregory.'

GAIL

Biggest problem? Attitude. My attitude. He tells me things—I don't listen. I want to do what I want to do—when I want to do it. He doesn't like that. So we argue. Then he gets mad and goes home. So then we start all over again the next day. We discuss it, and if that doesn't work, we call the whole thing quits—until I feel like talking to him.

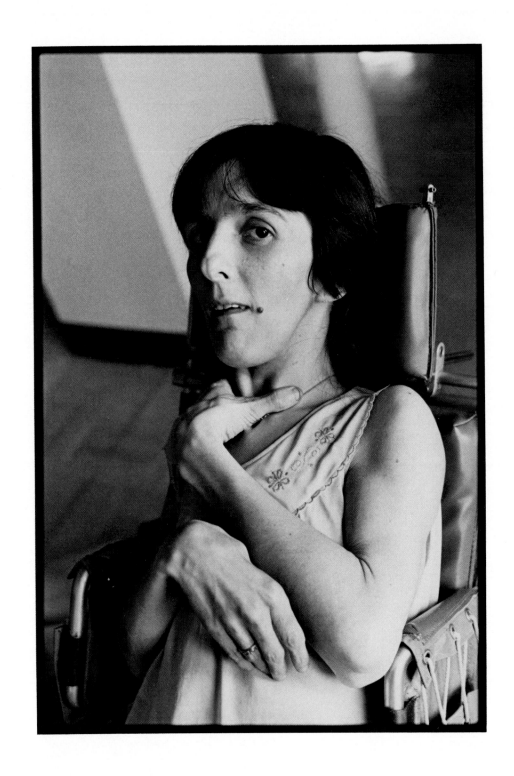

ANNE

ANNE

I fell in love with Jimmy—I knew him two and a
half years. I can't describe what Jimmy meant
to me. I never had *anybody* feeling about me
the way Jimmy did. . . . And that date that he
died [in 1977] . . . I felt like—boom!—my world
ended, really, without him. Like I had nothing to
live for. . . . I feel like there's nobody but me,
myself, and I—us three in our little corner of
our own world.

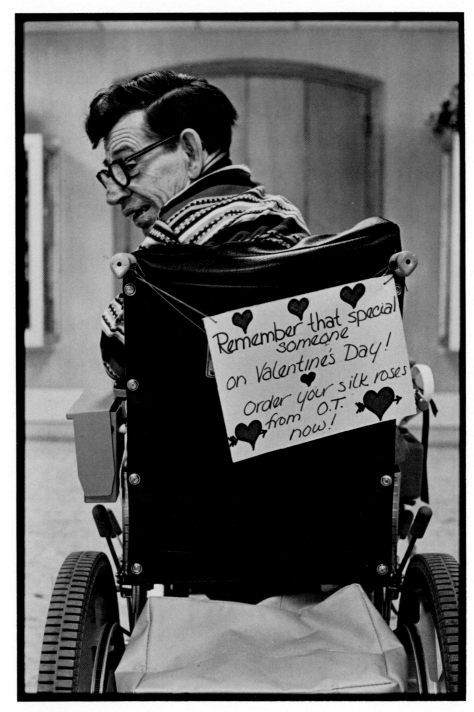

FRANK

PEGGY and DAVID

PEGGY AND DAVID

PEGGY

Is it too late for me to begin having a boyfriend? Ain't fifty a little late? We met square-dancing in Founder's Hall. . . . I haven't felt like this since I was a little girl—I'm up on cloud nine! Everything seems easy now. . . . When I was sixteen I hadn't been kissed. Dave is the first.

DAVID

Loving to be with someone. Like I am right now with Peggy. That's what it means to be in love.

PEGGY AND DAVID

PEGGY AND DAVID

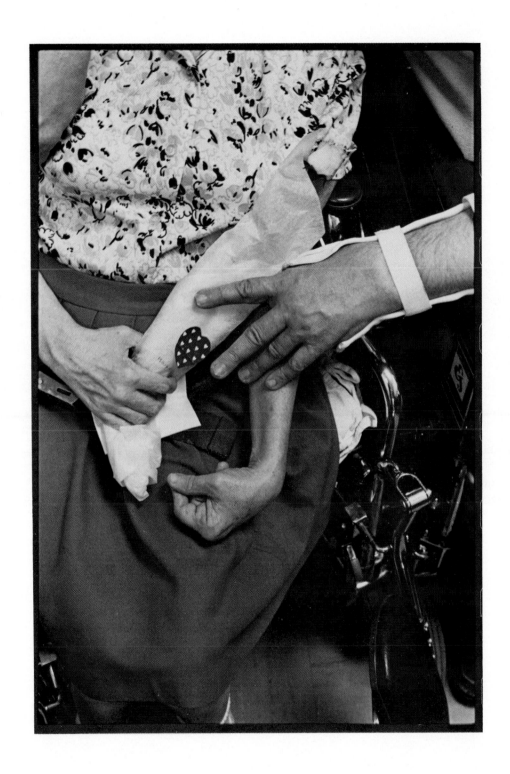

BILL and BETTY

MARY

DAVID and JO

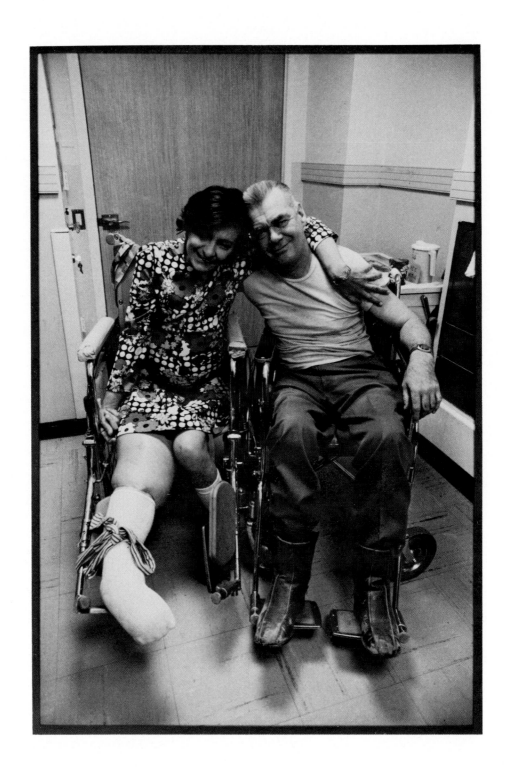

BILL

At first she looked gloomy, mouth down. She looked like an eight-ball in the side pocket. After we got talking and found we had something to share, she smiled. . . .

BETTY

He said he had to go down the Yellow Brick Road. And I asked him if I could go with him. So I could talk to him, to see if it would help any. He didn't let me at first.

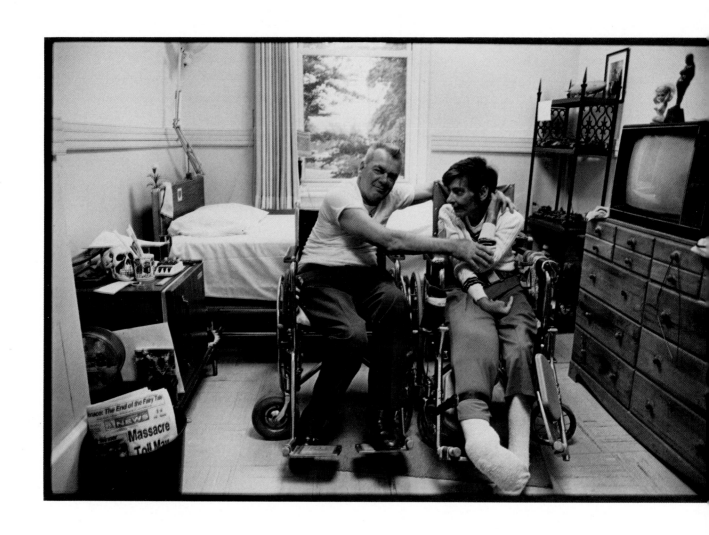

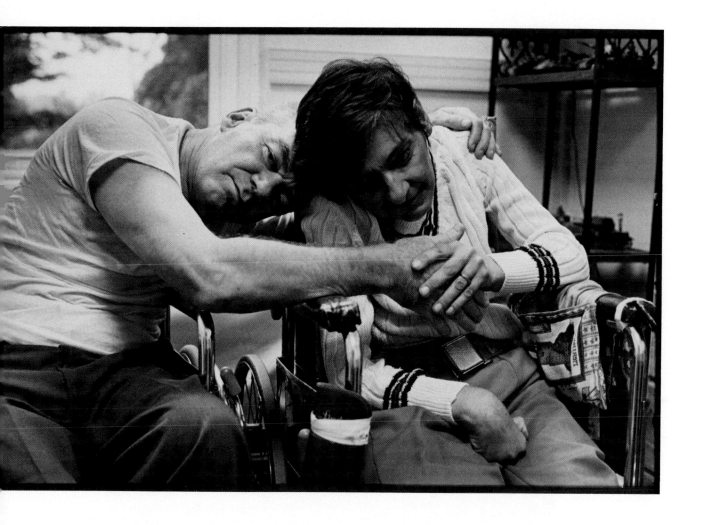

MARY

He [her husband, who died in May, 1982] used
to write poems by the beech tree we both
loved sitting under. He would look up at the
sky through the leaves and compare our love
to the sky—expansive and infinite. We would
go out there after lunch on a summer day and
sit there until after dinner. The light in the tree
was the sky playing a symphony, he used to
say, a symphony just for us. . . .

I think of the things he used to say, and it
gives me the strength to go on.

68

DAVID

I love her most dearly. . . . We have our problems—problems that all couples have—but
talk about them.

JO

We've been going together for twelve years.
He thinks I'm the most beautiful thing in the
world. Even if I look like God-knows-what, he
says I look beautiful. I'm his pride and joy. But
he can't get anybody else—what can he do?
But they don't know what they're missing—he's
a good buddy.

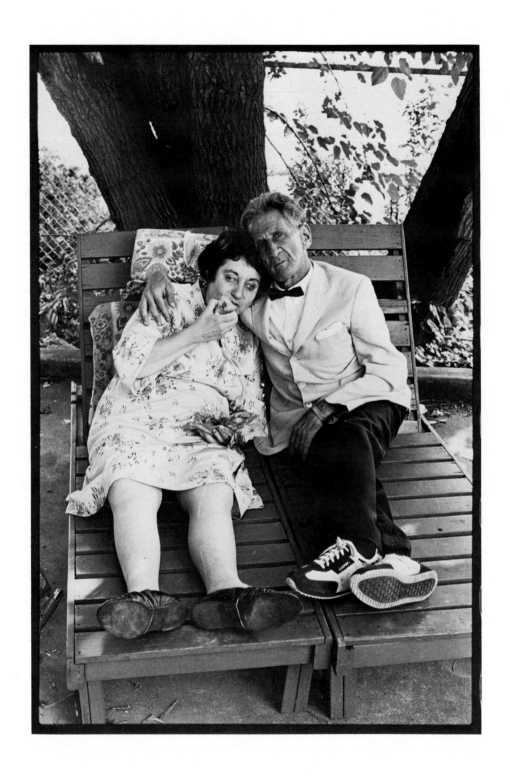

DAVID AND JO

THREE

TONY

DAWN and SAL

EARL

TONY

Like, one mornin'—five o'clock in the mornin',
right—we're both tired, right, but we're havin' a
good time. And we're talkin', and we're bein'
funny, right? So she comes out and asks me if
I think she's too forward. So, jokin' around, I
say, 'Yeah'—you know? And she got *highly* up-
set, and walked out of my van [which he got
shortly after moving into Inglis House] and left!
And didn't talk to me for two weeks! Now *that's*
no reason to get mad. . . . All stupid stuff she
gets mad at. In a way, I'm glad now that it's
over.

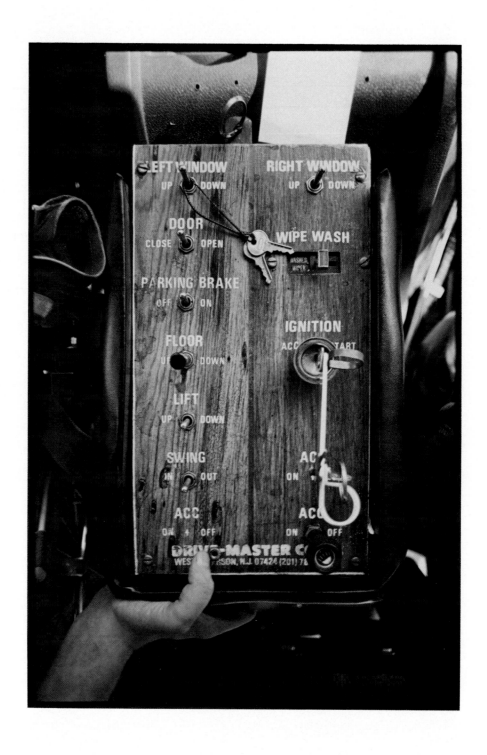

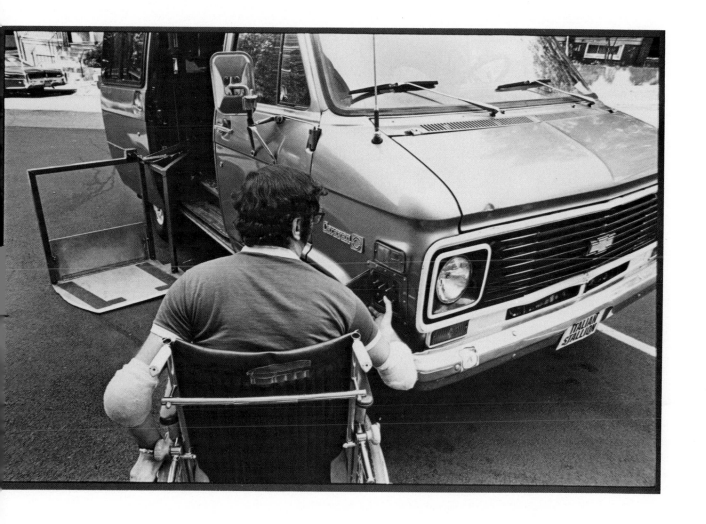

TONY

DAWN

I've had a better relationship with Sal than I ever had [with any man] before I was injured. . . . He knows the true Me.

SAL

Most people who are out-going before they become quads are out-going afterwards as well. . . . We're both hustlers, out-going people. We're doers, not watchers.

EARL

She [Shirley, a nurse] was here for four
months, during the summer of 1951. . . . When
she worked here, she'd always stop and say
goodnight to me before she went home. I loved
that. . . . I loved her . . . [but] she got married—
in 1954, I'm not sure. . . . They were married
only two years, and were divorced. Then, one
day, about ten years later, I called her up on
the phone, and she said: 'I got married again,
and I have a baby.' And that's the last time I
talked to her. . . . I love her. She knows I love
her. She loved me, too. . . . That's about all I
can tell you. That's the story.

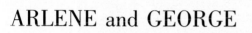

ARLENE and GEORGE

GEORGE

I have the same feelings toward her now as I did then [twenty-one years ago when they were married]. I feel 90 percent of the same feelings as I did then . . . maybe 85 percent. There's one area of our lives that we can't master—and that's why we're apart.

ARLENE

I still love him, but I have to put up with his—
. . . he wants a life of his own because he says that one day he is going to find the perfect girl, non-handicapped, and drift off with her to I-don't-know-what. . . .

ARLENE AND GEORGE

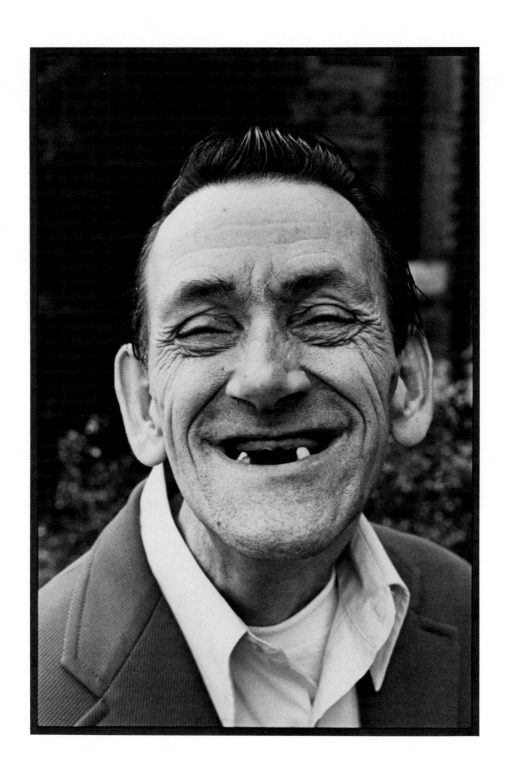

ARLENE AND GEORGE

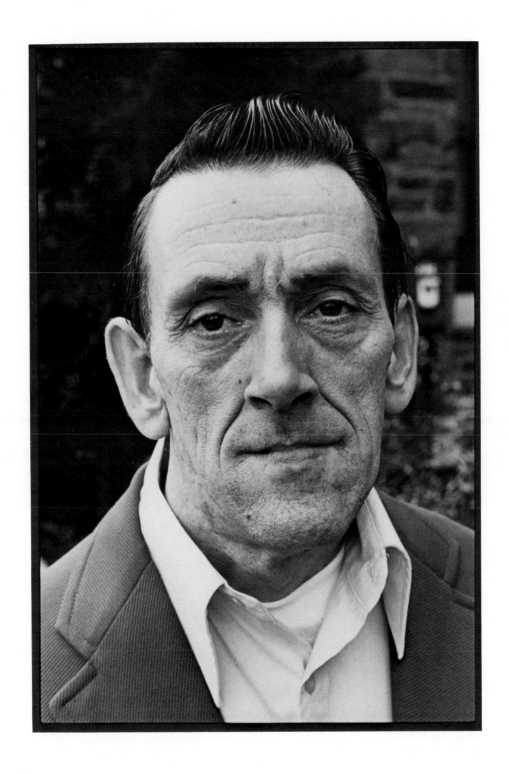

ARLENE AND GEORGE

ARLENE AND GEORGE

ARLENE AND GEORGE

DAVID and LINDA

PERRY and MYRA

ALICE and DONALD

CAROL

HUGH

JOHN and GAIL

DAVID AND LINDA

LINDA

I've known David all my life. . . . We grew up together, and he went his way and I went my way [in her case, a marriage that ended after fifteen years]. I've always admired him—he's always been my best friend. And, you know, to have a relationship you have to be a friend first. . . . It's been a year this past November [1981] that we've been married. . . .

DAVID

The thing that we have going for us that makes it [commitment to each other] a little easier, I think, is that we have a common faith in God. Our marriage is a triangle: it's my relationship with God, and His relationship with me, reflected in my relationship with her. And her relationship with God reflected back with me. . . . Linda's able to do that a lot better than I am—letting God, you know, run the show. I have a lot of problems sometimes. . . . I want to be the big Me. I want to be The Answer to the Whole Thing. You have to let God do that.

MYRA

For twenty-five years I was married to my husband [he died in 1972]. He *never* said, 'I like you' . . . 'I *love* you.' *Never.* Unh-uhh. *He* [nodding toward Perry] tells me I'm beautiful. After he met me, the next day he called me and he said, '*You* are the most gorgeous woman in town!' I said, '*You* are full of shit!'

PERRY

My wife died of leukemia [in 1974] and I had to take care of her—and, in those days, you couldn't get insurance for cancer patients, and I spent every cent I had for nurses around-the-clock and hospital. . . .

I first met Myra at a singles' dance seven years ago [in 1975]. That was before she was sick [multiple sclerosis, diagnosed in 1979]. She thought I was Italian, but I'm not—I'm Jewish. And I thought *she* was Italian, but she's Jewish! It was love at first sight. . . . Her psychiatrist said I'm giving her something that her husband didn't give her. I can't come every day [to Inglis House, which Myra entered in May, 1982], but I come on weekends and all holidays. I call her on the phone three or four times a day when I'm home. . . . And I taught her that—you know, years ago when a person masturbated it was a sin; today it *isn't*—and I

even showed her how to masurbate herself when we're not together. It's not a sin. Even a *psychiatrist* will tell you that it's normal. . . .

You oughta see her when she has make-up on. Even with her illness it's a different thing, but she's not able to do it now—and *I* can't put the make-up on her, you know what I mean? But when we go to the Marriott [her two sons treated them to an overnight special each New Year's Eve before she died in 1983] since she's not able to put make-up on and all, her sons see that the make-up shop there and a hairdresser shop make her up the way she was when she was well. Last year [1981] she was home, sick, but we still—she wasn't as bad off as she is now—I still had to take care of her [on] account of her condition, when she messes, when she can't help herself—we still went to the Marriott and she had a terrific time on New Year's. Even though she couldn't dance, I talked to the head waiter and they got her a table right near the band . . . and she danced with her hands. She *loves* music. So do I.

ALICE AND DONALD

ALICE

I'm a lot older than Donald—twenty-five years.
. . . Going with somebody has nothing to do
with anything physical, and I feel that the more
people learned this it would be a better world.
. . . We never hold hands—maybe I'll just touch
him like that [grazes his arm with her hand].
. . . We may be funny, but we get along very
well.

DONALD

I have spinal muscular cerebral atrophy; it
causes a weakness in the leg muscles. Now I
am no longer able to get out of the chair. . . . I
try to do for Alice whatever I can despite this—
like reach down and adjust her pedals. She
gives me shaves with my electric razor.

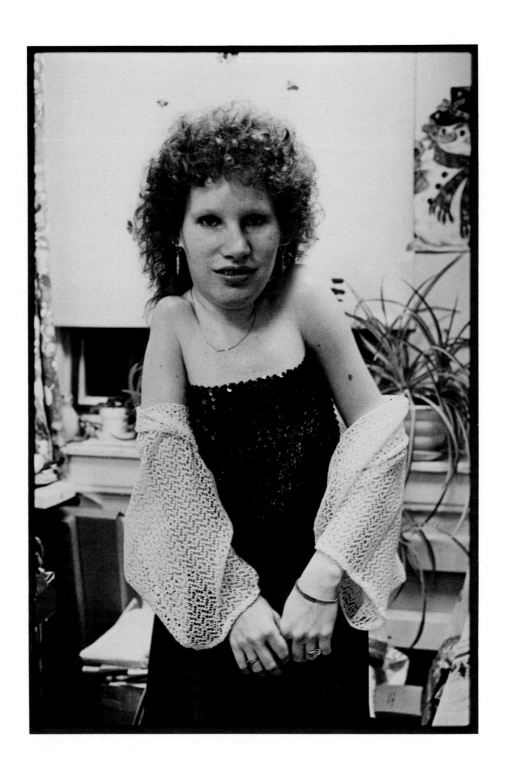

CAROL

[Chose not to be interviewed. Photographed in her room, New Year's Eve, 1982, awaiting the arrival of her date.]

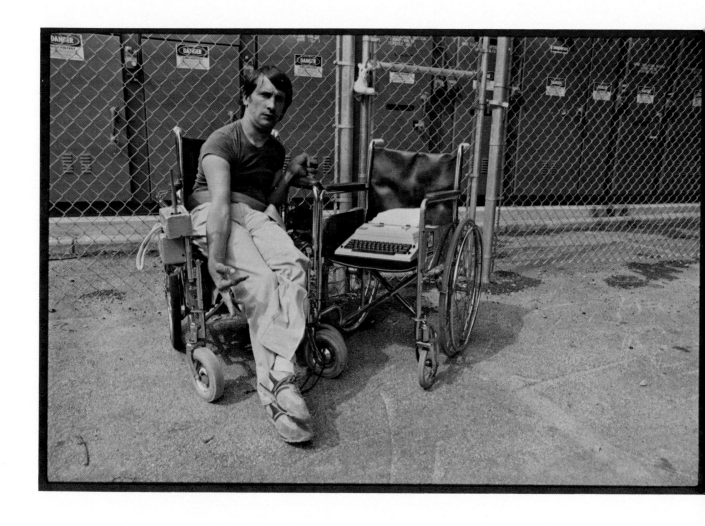

To love a typewriter, how ridiculous
what insanity, how sick, unreal
the idea sounds absurd, but it's true
I must be mad, loving a machine
having an affair with nuts and bolts
I must have gone mad, totally deranged
to deviate from the norm like this
but I don't care, I really don't
whenever we make love it's electra

Hugh

JOHN

I've made mistakes with this word. In the past, a *lot* of mistakes with the word 'commitment.' . . . What I mean by 'commitment' basically comes down to this: I love Gail, and I give to Gail, but you have to get in return sometimes in order to give—you know what I mean? As a person, I cannot give and not get back anything—because of the way I am and the way my life has been. . . . I am a person who cannot give unless I get something in return. . . .

GAIL

He [Gregory] wanted a commitment, and I wouldn't give it to him—because I don't want to be tied down to nobody. The right person . . . maybe I will commit myself. But Gregory wasn't the right person. Neither's John. He's a nice guy—that's all. The only thing I don't like is that he asks too many questions—questions that don't concern him—like why I go out with other people. I say, 'None of your business.' But he just asks more questions.

FOUR

PRISCILLA and BOB

HE and SHE, No. 1

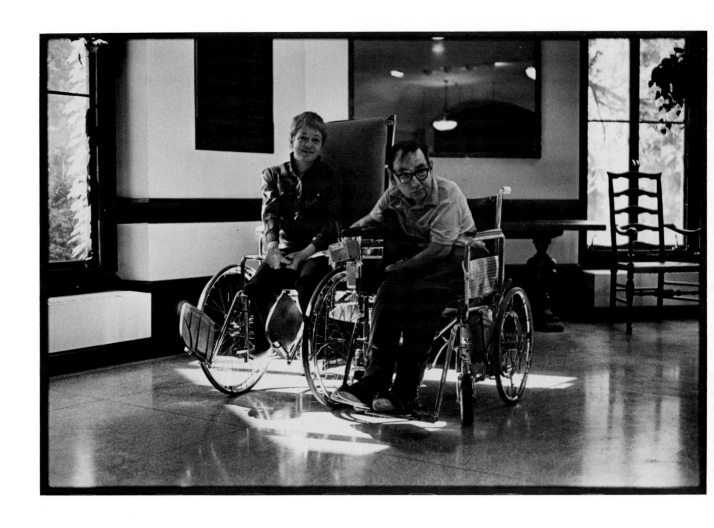

PRISCILLA

I L–O–V–E B–O–B–B–Y. I L–O–V–E
H–I–S P–R–E–T–T–Y B–R–O–W–N E–Y–E–S.
I–F I T–A–L–K, B–O–B–B–Y H–E–A–R–S M–E.
I T–A–L–K– L–O–V–E W–I–T–H M–Y
H–A–N–D–S.

BOB

She means a heck of a lot to me. . . . I have
learned her way of communication. I have
learned the motion of what she's trying to say.
. . . She can't speak; her motions do the speak-
ing for her. She can get through to *me* where
some people won't take the time. . . .

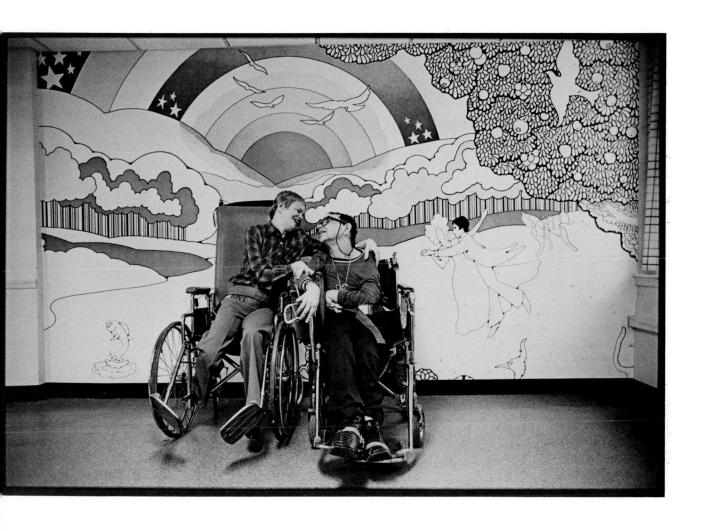

HE AND SHE, NO. 1

HE

We don't take anything for granted. Things can change too suddenly in life. I was walking one minute, the next minute I was paralyzed from the waist down [he was in a car accident]; in her case, it was a little girl who was walking [she developed muscular dystrophy].

I know [she] is the woman I want to spend my life with. Without her there's something *lacking*, something very *major* lacking—and that's just the way I feel.

SHE

As [he] and I have often said, we feel sorry for other couples who have never *known* in any way what we have known in just *three* years or more. We've already had more than some people have ever known in their lifetime. He's got sensitivity, virility, sexuality that your so-called 'normal' guys *never* possessed. . . . He's got everything, every strength that I think anyone could ask for, and I feel sorry for those people who are always *floundering* in their relationships, their jealousies, their mistrusts. We *don't know* that nonsense because *our* feeling is so intensified by the knowledge [that] tomorrow we might—one of us might—be sick and die. We *both* know how sick we can get . . . so we've got to pack a lot in. . . . We knew the precariousness of existence *before* we met, but we have that much more to lose now. . . .

[Couple chose not to be identified photographically except by these pictures of her room.]

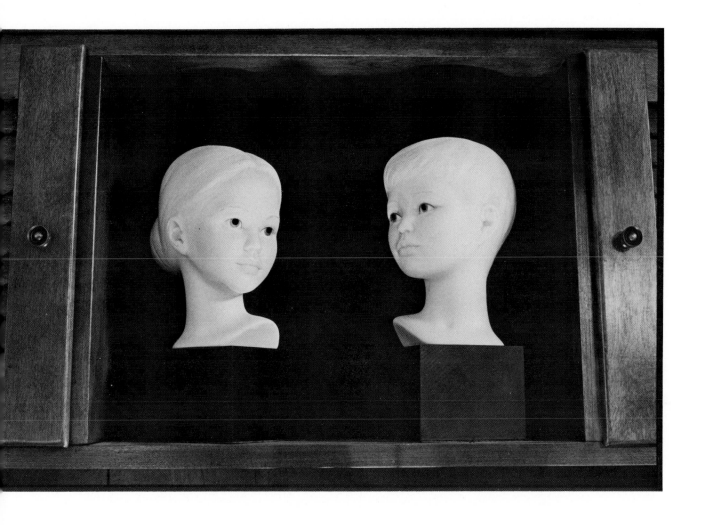

HE AND SHE, NO. 1

MURRAY and FRANCES

MURRAY AND FRANCES

MURRAY

When I married Frances, I swore that I would stay with her till death do us part, see, and I'm keeping my word—that's all. This is what I wanted; now, I wouldn't want any other woman. Even if she'd give me a divorce today, I wouldn't want any other woman. I've had a marvelous—a *beautiful*—life with her, even with her handicaps. She's humorous, she's smart— and we talk the same language: we don't even have to come out with the exact words. I can say *one word* and she knows what I'm thinking about . . . because [of] living with me that length of time [fifty years of marriage, the last thirty-five with her multiple sclerosis—the last fifteen of these at Inglis House]. I come here four or five times a week. Her love *draws* me out here. When I come here, I feel *good*; I look for the moment when I have to get in the car to come out here.

So it must be *in me* to want to do that. And we can have an argument; we can have a difference of opinion. And I can leave her in a huff here, but the next time I come—it's just like nothing happened. And I daren't walk in that room without kissing her! . . . So, we're still on our honeymoon, even though she's incapacitated to the point where she's not really a *wife* to me. But as far as a companion? She's all I want. So, that's the way it is. . . . Yep.

FRANCES

I know there are a lot of things to be thankful for . . . but after all there are women here whose husbands just put them in here and *forgot* about them. And I think that's sad. In fact, when I told my husband how *worried* I was about him once when he wasn't feeling well, he said, 'Don't worry'—not to 'worry about me'— and all that business—and I said to him: 'Don't you *dare* deprive me of that! That's one of my *privileges*.' The people for whom I feel sorry are the people that have nobody to worry about. . . . It's a reciprocal thing.

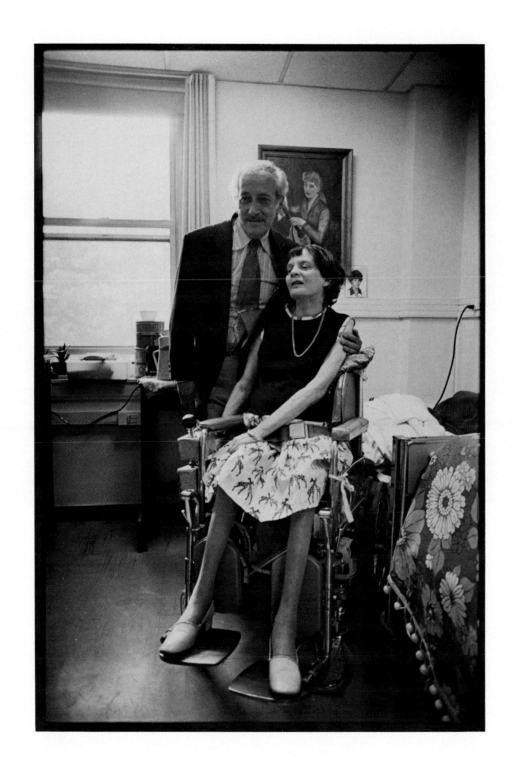

EMILY and DON

ANDREA

ANDY and CAROL

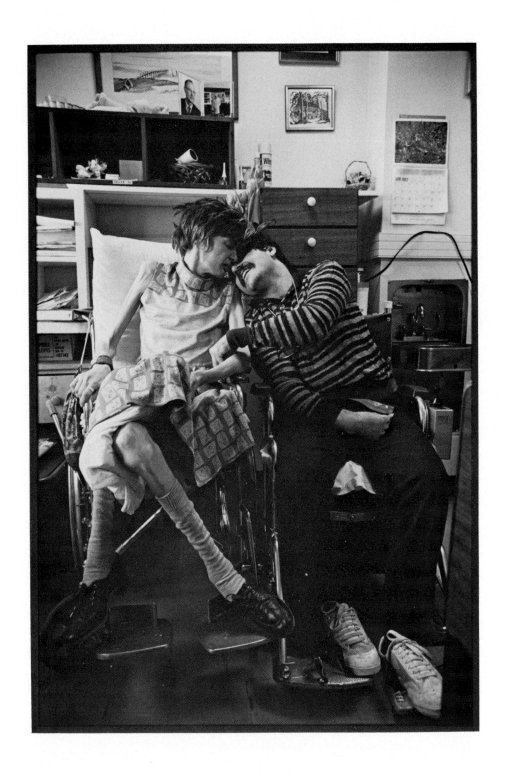

EMILY

You know what he did? I was in the hospital for two or three weeks before I came back here . . . he got out of his own wheelchair and gave it to me—an electric wheelchair. . . .

I'm fifty-one and he's thirty-two. . . . [Age] doesn't have a damn thing to do with being in love. . . .

DON

She's fifty-one and I'm thirty-two . . . I love her as a mother. I love touching her. . . . [Turning to Emily:] I should be on the other side. ['Why?' she asks.] Because I'm left-handed now [since the motorcycle accident]. . . .

EMILY AND DON

ANDREA

I need understanding and freedom to do whatever I want with my life. I am a loving person, but everything I say comes out wrong in his eyes [her husband, from whom she was separated at the time]. . . . I miss that very loving person that I knew before. I told him I don't know him anymore. I used to know him like a book, but not no more. He doesn't open up to me at all. . . .

[Husband chose not to be photographed or interviewed.]

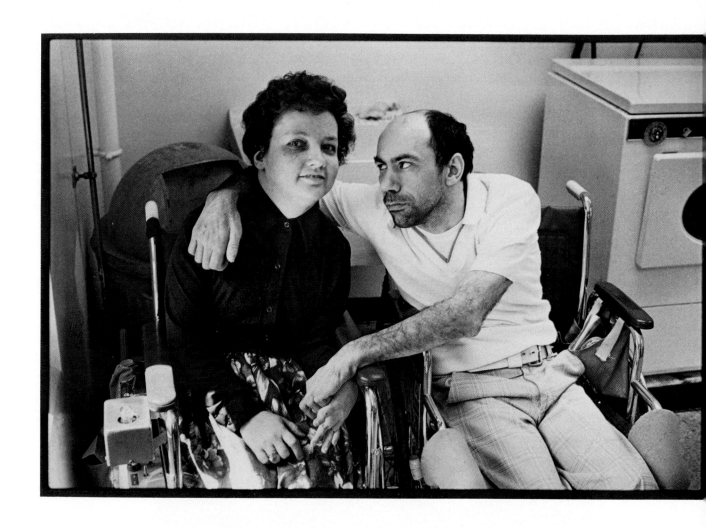

ANDY AND CAROL

ANDY

For a while, sure I felt bad [about breaking up with Lois] but I went on and picked myself up, and I feel this [relationship with Carol] will be better for me. . . . It's doing me a lot of good so far, and I hope that she feels that way. . . . For me, I don't want to lose her. . . .

CAROL

I'm looking for the same thing he's looking for—security. I thought I had it in the past, but I didn't. [Security is] being with each other and having the ability to talk to one another. . . .

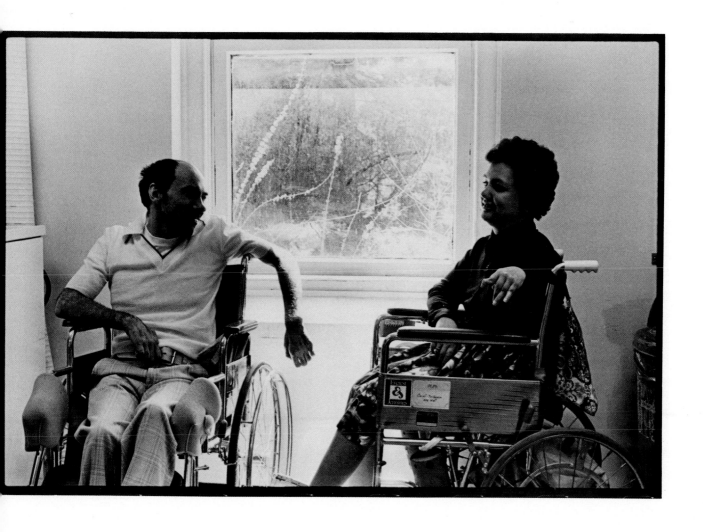

ANDY AND CAROL

FIVE

HE

ISABELLE and CHARLIE

HE and SHE, NO. 2

DIANE

BARBARA

GREGORY

HE

I have to keep what private life I have *private*. I can't be too obvious [about his bi-sexuality], or the lack of sexual preference will destroy me. I have to keep a low profile, sexually, in order to survive within a place like this. . . . I'm good at the game. ['How do you keep a low sexual profile? What does that mean?'] It means not losing control of your dignity and sleeping with just anybody who wants you. You survive by creating an image of something you're not, which, in my case, would be creating a somewhat macho image.

[Chose to be identified only by image of himself which he constructed, with photographer's aid, on opposite page.]

ISABELLE

We both like Elvis. And we both like Dolly Parton. . . . He has a Fonz shirt, I got an Elvis shirt. We tease each other about Fonz—you know, Fonzie? sticks his thumbs up?—you know, on 'Happy Days'—you seen it, didn't ya? So that's what we do: I see Charlie, I go 'Hey-y-y-y-y!'

He's a sweet guy. . . . When I'm with him we talk—and we always find something to talk about. At least *I* do, because I'm a *motor* mouth! I never shut up. . . . What else is there to say? He's friendly, he's happy and cheerful, he's . . . he's—*nice*! What is there *not* to like about Charlie? My mother thinks the world of him.

CHARLIE

She's a good kid.

HE

'I am a 52-year-old male with cerebral palsy and I have a wonderful girlfriend about my age. We are both on Supplemental Security Income [SSI] due to our disabilities. I get $283 per month and she gets $293 since she came out of the nursing home. We are both very religious people and we want to be married according to God's law, but the Federal Government is saying we cannot do it because if we do, they will only give us a total of $300 per month. Furthermore, I found out through my district office that even if we don't marry and if I introduce her as my wife, they will take away our money and our rights anyhow. . . . It is due to such inequities that people who have been married for 50 or 60 years are being divorced so that they will have money to pay for the bare necessities of life. . . . I am begging you for help so that we can keep God's commandments.'*

SHE

'We have the same thoughts and feelings as others do. We feel angry. And deprived of love. We see other couples who are happy so why can't we be happy too? My fiance and I love each other so very much. Why can't SSI help us? I don't see why they can't. Is there a law against happiness for us?'*

*Excerpted from a letter to a public official in Philadelphia several months before the couple, who choose to remain unidentified, went ahead and got married. Photograph was taken outside the hall where their reception was held.

DIANE

I got angry with him [her husband] for putting
me in here [five years ago]. But, see, at home
he said I needed nursing care, and he couldn't
afford the nurse anymore. . . . I felt that when I
was home I could handle the house. I cleaned
it—it's a seven-room house with two bath-
rooms. I kept it clean and I cooked every day.
Of course, it took me time. I fell many times
trying to hang clothes down the basement. I
had a dryer, but there are some things you
want to hang up, before you dry them, not to
get them too wrinkled—like his shirts. . . . So
when I call him up, he's busy washing clothes.
I say, 'Well, if I was home, I could do it for you'
. . . although I don't know if—I can't walk, *stand*
like I did then [due to multiple sclerosis].

[Husband chose not to be photographed or interviewed.]

BARBARA

BARBARA

I didn't think. You see, I was having sex with so
many guys *before* and I didn't *get* that way
[pregnant]—that's why I thought I could never
get pregnant. I didn't really expect it. It was
like a shock to *me*, too. [She's about four
months' pregnant at time of photograph.] I
didn't think *I could.* . . .

He denied the whole thing. I told him it
was his baby. He denies it. But it *is.* . . . I think
that men just want what they can get. . . . They
get girls pregnant and don't want to take the
responsibility. They just want to 'do it.' That's
the way I feel. I didn't feel that way before I got
pregnant, though. I didn't think about it much.
. . . I didn't think about *anything* much before I
got pregnant. Now all I can think about is
being pregnant. Where I'm gonna go from the
hospital. . . . I'm not getting hope from anybody, really. It's kind of discouraging, [but] I'm
still determined to keep [the baby] if I can.

GREGORY

She [Gail] said she wanted her *freedom*. She said that would make her *happy*. So I was talking to her over the phone [several months after they broke up], so I said, what did she learn? She said she has her freedom, but she's not satisfied now—she's still unhappy. And I don't understand why she's still unhappy. She got what she wanted. . . .

I got a lot more patience [from being with Gail]. I wasn't really a very patient person, and that's what I really needed. And I still need a lot more. In Gail, I saw myself—the way I used to be. That's why I stayed so long. . . . Hopefully, we'll remain friends.

DAWN and BILL

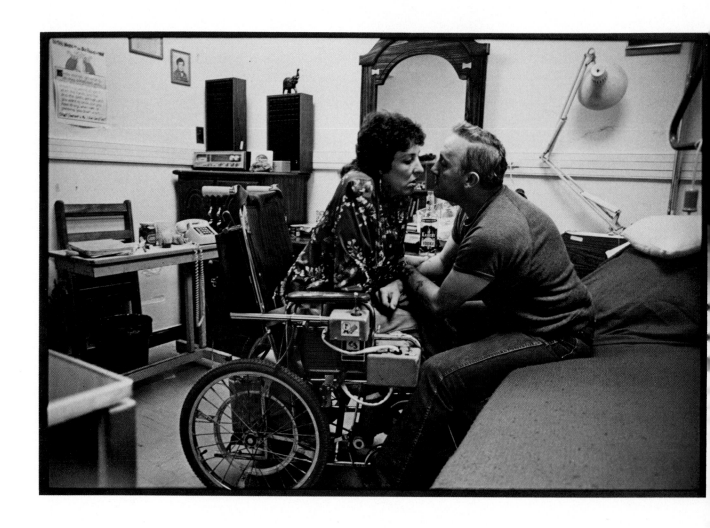

DAWN

He has only known me one way—and that's
disabled [paraplegia]. He didn't know me when
I was walking, so he's bound to be taking me
for the person that I *am*. . . .

    Not only do I love him, he's the greatest
friend I've ever had. We've talked about each
other's life—about things that have hurt him in
life, and things that have hurt me. We both had
bad marriages. We spend almost every night
together; it's that type of relationship where we
would be together a lot more, too, if I wasn't
living here where the visiting hours are over at
nine o'clock. . . . We get frustrated, but we
have our times alone together. . . .

[Bill chose not to be interviewed.]

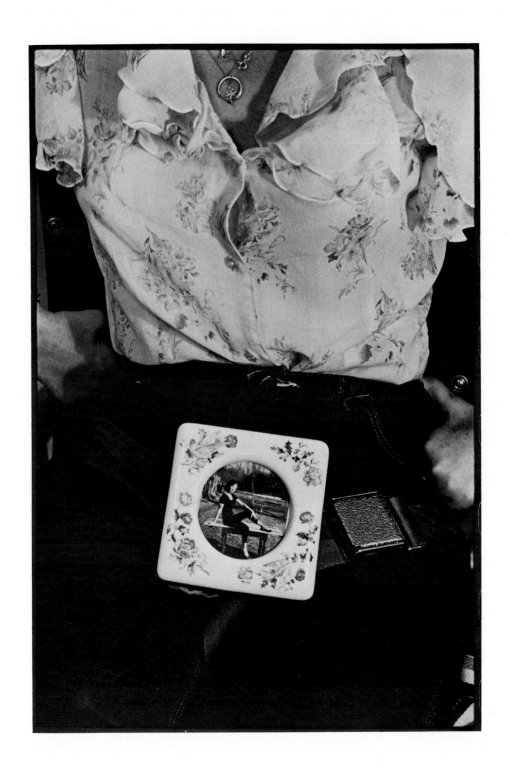

DAWN AND BILL

STEVE and HUGH

SAM

RAYMOND and CHARLENE

ANNE and BETTY

STEVE (r.)

We take each other as full individuals. We have, I think one of the most remarkable relationships that I've ever been a part of because there's no *demands*, you know, there's no *you musts* on anybody's side. . . . I don't have to be *strong* or in any sense 'in control' for him to respect me as a human being. And I don't take it as a 'given' that he is always strong or capable or even always *caring*; I mean, that's one of the reasons that we *argue* so much—because there's such a freedom of expression between us that anything that is said is all right. There are no signposts that say: You Cannot Say This, or You Cannot Do That—or whatever. It's like he doesn't make any demands on me *other than* expressing the fact that he wishes me to be *as happy* as possible, you know. I mean . . . if I'm being a little lazy or, you know, something like that, he doesn't 'push'; he just suggests stuff. . . . Sometimes I—I've told you a little that I write—when I get lazy like that [about his writing], he sits there and says, 'Well, you're not using the gifts God gave you.' Something like that, you know—not in those words *exactly*, because Hugh never talks like that. But he gets down into it and he says, like, 'You really need to be doing this right now because it'll help you with *this* depression, *that* problem—whatever—and doesn't *ever* make any conditions. . . .

HUGH

Steve is somebody I can go to, and he tolerates my 'insanity.' He lets me cry on his shoulder—which has been a mite soggy as of late. He's my friend, and I love him. That's it.

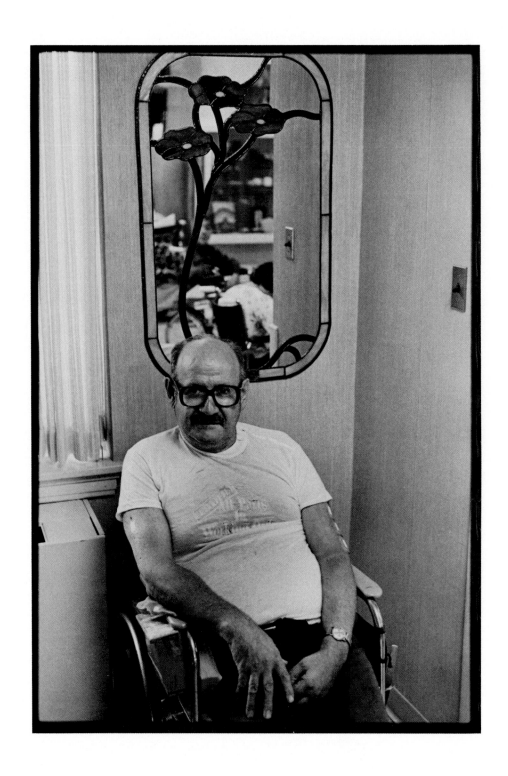

SAM

She [his wife] had a hard life—MS [multiple sclerosis]. We just unveiled her stone. It's a double stone—that's where I'll be; they've got a piece of ground waiting for me. About forty people came out to honor her. . . . We celebrated our fortieth wedding anniversary last year [June, 1980]. She left me with five children that are grand, and three grand children—that's how I like to put it. We had a cookout at my son's place. They brought out a cake that had the crown that was on our wedding cake—it had been stored in a cedar chest for forty years! Our daughter sprung it on us—we didn't know it existed. . . .

[Photographed in lobby in front of mirror his son made and donated to Inglis House.]

RAYMOND AND CHARLENE

RAYMOND

Actually, to me, it don't mean anything [the twenty-four-year difference in their ages]. She's female, and I'm male. And we love to be with each other. It don't mean anything, as far as I'm concerned—just as long as we're happy together.

CHARLENE

Who cares!?

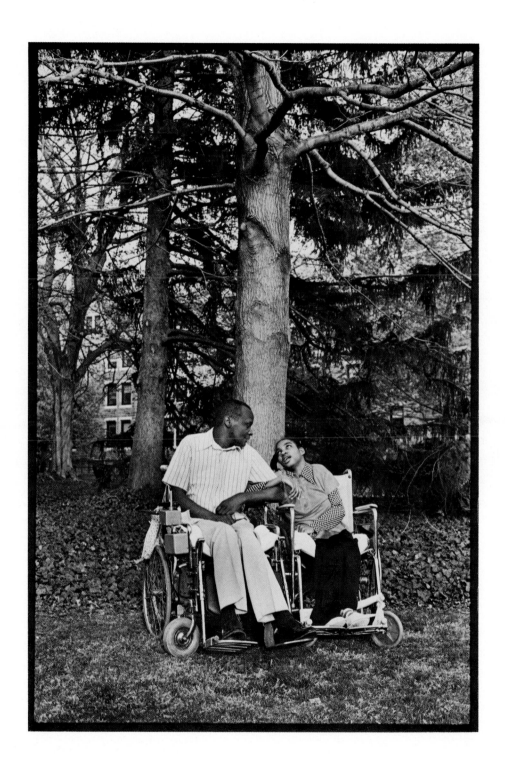

RAYMOND AND CHARLENE

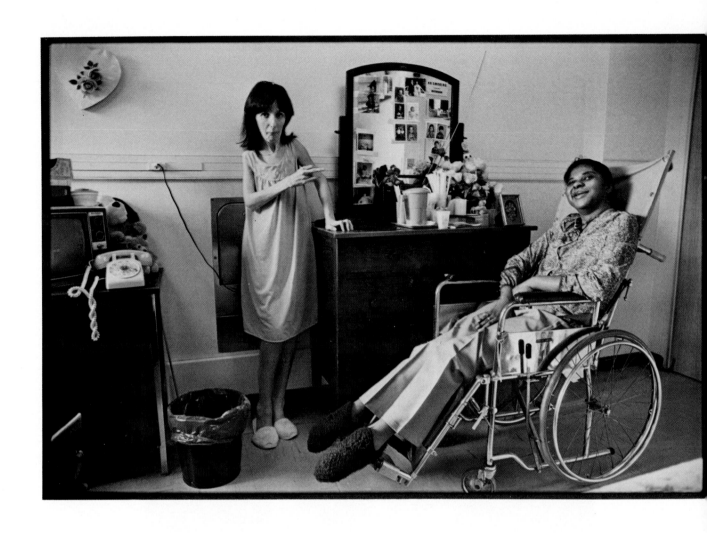

ANNE (l.)

There's no parting me and Betty: wherever Betty goes, I go; wherever I go, Betty goes. Really. . . . Every morning I holler over to her room, 'Good morning, Betty!' And she hollers over to me, 'Good morning, Annie, how are you?' And then she gets up, you know, or if I get up before her, I go over to her room and she's in bed and we talk for awhile, and then I leave, and then when the nurse does her, and when she gets up, she comes out in the hallway, and if I'm out in the hallway, then we talk. Then, two o'clock, I come back to my room, get out of my chair, and she might, you know, wiggle herself over here, and we talk, and then she goes back in her room by three—she usually goes to bed by quarter-to-four—and that's, you know, that's our day.

BETTY

She just seems like a regular person.

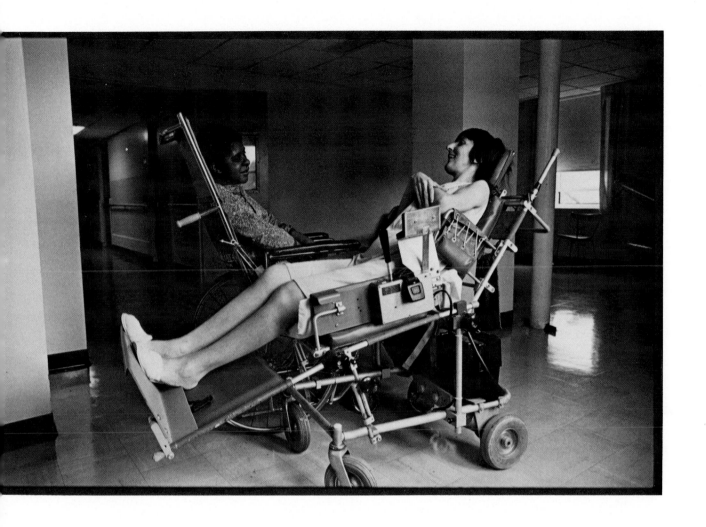

SIX

AL and BEV

GINA and EARL

AL

She means everything to me. . . . As soon as I get my divorce—put this in the book!—I'll marry her.

BEV

No matter how good or bad the situation is, he's there for me, loving me—letting me know he loves me. . . . Like everything else, you have to find your own way of intimacy. There's nothing that I can give to Al that he can't give back to me. It's mutual.

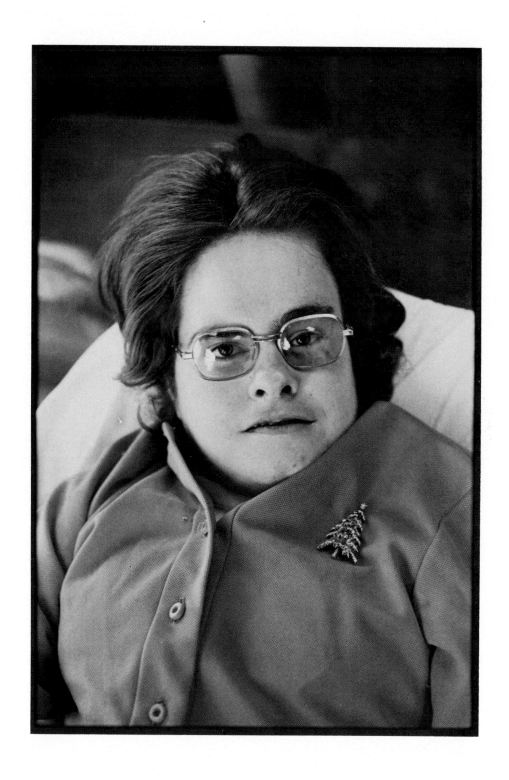

AL AND BEV

EARL

Some people don't look at it [an older person's sex life] that way [as important and healthy]. 'Oh, that dirty, dirty old man!' [he's sixty-five, she's thirty-three]—I'm sick and tired of listening to that 'dirty old man!' talk! I think it's wrong when they say that. What the man needs is *love*, just like I'm giving Gina. Love makes me feel happier. But a lot of people don't understand it because not only am I older—I'm handicapped. I say to hell with that! Handicap or no handicap, we're all *human*. We're *all* human. . . .

GINA

Above all, he has an inner strength in him that has reflected on me and gotten through to me so that I'm more able to cope with life. He has a much better inner strength than I have seen in any other person. . . . I can talk to him about anything and everything under the sun, and he can make me feel *so* much better and so much more at ease.

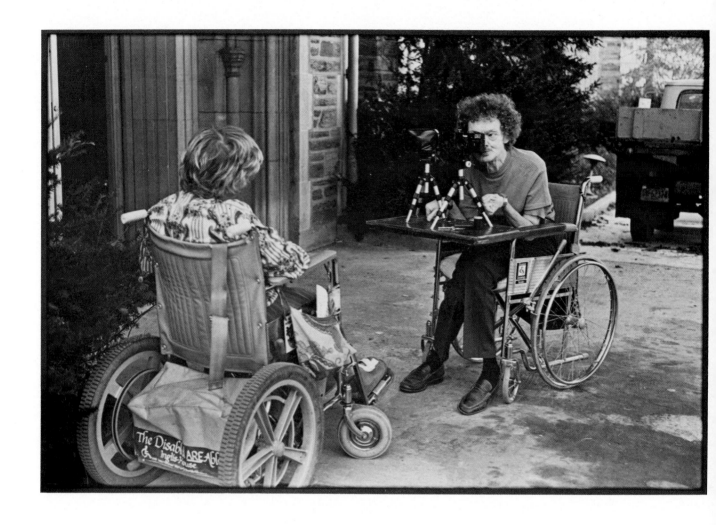

BUDDY and RUTH

BUDDY

Believe it or not, we were boyfriend and girl-friend in 1958–59 . . . but we broke up [he married another woman in 1961; she died in 1971]. I'm a member of HEC—Handicapped Encounter Christ. About six months ago, we had a three-day retreat, and I went on it, and to my surprise—I almost fainted when I saw her—there was Ruth! She said that even though it's been more than twenty years, she's never stopped loving me. I said, 'How about starting over?' . . . We're both older now and we know what we want. And we're going to get it: companionship and love.

RUTH

He is the most considerate person I have ever known. He thinks of *everything* to make me comfortable. . . . As a woman? He makes me feel like I'm something special. . . . Sensuality is very important. Because if we didn't touch each other we couldn't feel how much we love each other. . . .

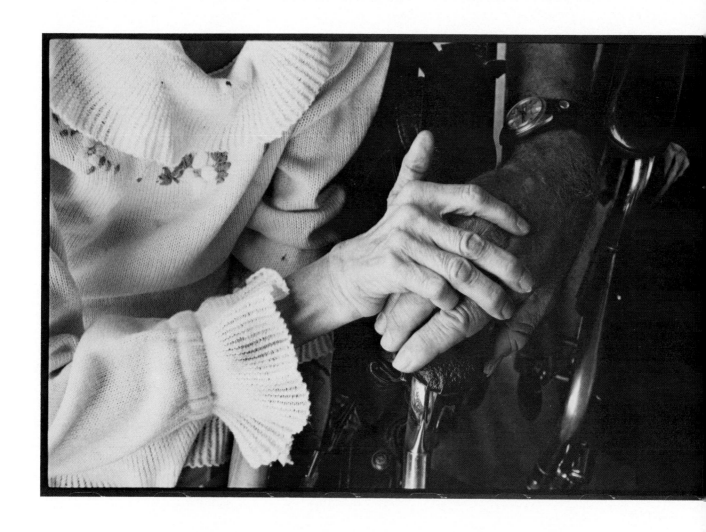

ROSEMARIE and GEORGE

JOHN and GAIL

TED

SOL and KAY

LOIS

ELEANOR and CARL

ROSEMARIE AND GEORGE

ROSEMARIE

When I first went with George, he was known as an Inglis House 'wolf,' and I figured, you know, this man wants to go with me, and how can I trust him? . . . When I have a boyfriend—that's the One-and-Only. This man likes *everybody*! So why am I going into it? And I figured, well, we all have to take a chance in our life, so this is the chance I'll take. And I can honestly, truthfully say: in fourteen years he only went out of line *once*—which he has regretted, and has apologized [for]—and I took him back. Everybody at Inglis House thought I was *crazy*—of course, the whole hall knew about it—but I thought: it was *my* life, and I'll take another chance. After all, what is life all about? Chances. . . . But he'll never get the *second* chance if it happens again!

GEORGE

I think that companionship is a great, great thing because when you have someone you can depend on, and rely on, that's what I call . . . love. Rosie means to me—well, I don't know how to put it—but I wouldn't trade her for every other girl here, any woman here. . . . She gives me love, she gives me her attention—well, she just gives me everything that a man needs, and that's saying a hell of a lot, right? So you can take it from there, right?

JOHN AND GAIL

JOHN

It wasn't as . . . uh—what's the word I'm looking for—it wasn't as *romantic* [proposing to
Gail] as I would have liked it to have been. I
just have known for three months before I got
engaged to Gail—I knew I wanted to spend the
rest of my life with her. And I knew that in this
day and age you have to take good experiences when they come; you have to take good
relationships when they come. You can't be
picky about it. You *can* be picky, but *I know*
that Gail is the one who I want because I love
her from the bottom of my heart. And although
it wasn't the way—although the proposal wasn't
the way I wanted it . . . in other words, I wanted
to take her out to dinner, share a bottle of wine,
and then pop the question. But since I'm not—
since I'm not a wealthy man!—we had to settle
for Pizza Town food, and the radio, and soda.

And I guess what I'm basically trying to
say is, although when I came in here [to Inglis
House in 1981 at age eighteen], I was pretty
immature—and to this day I may still act a little
bit immature—I feel that I've grown up a lot,
and I know I'm going to have to pull away from
my family some day, but not totally; but if I
want to pull away from my family *at all*, I have
to be with someone I love. And Gail is that
person.

GAIL

As soon as I get enough money to get out of
[here], I'm gone! I've been here for six years;
as soon as we get enough money, I'm splittin'!
['After you're married, where will you live?']
Here, for about a year. We have some re-
searching to do [regarding government-
subsidized housing on the West Coast, somewhere near John's family, where they hope to
live together] . . .

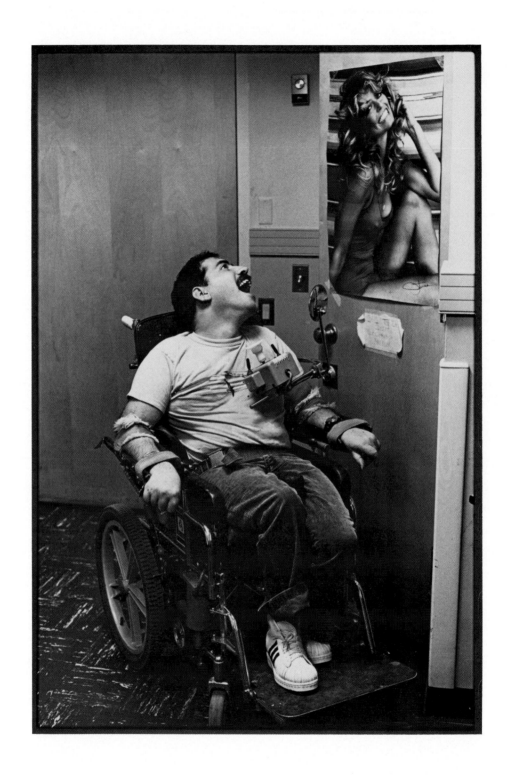

TED

TED

Q: . . . *Did you say goodbye to each other before you left that institution* [seven years before entering Inglis House]?

A: [Eyes blinking = Yes] Yes.

Q: *Was she handicapped?*

A: [Tongue protruding = No] No.

Q: *Was this institution outside Philadelphia?*

A: Yes.

Q: *More than a hundred miles away?*

A: Yes.

Q: [Responding to his sideward head-movement:] *You want me to get something out of your bag* [behind his wheelchair]?

A: Yes.

Q: *Your address book?*

A: Yes.

Q: [I thumb through the address book, naming places; he sticks his tongue out each time until:] *'Johnstown, PA?' She's from Johnstown?*

A: Yes. Yes.

Q: [I read her name aloud as Ted smiles deeply and keeps blinking. I see no phone number listed.] *Does she have a phone?*

A: No.

Q: *Does she ever write to you?*

A: No.

Q: *You were her boyfriend—and she was your girlfriend—for two years?*

A: Yes.

Q: *Have you ever written a letter to her?*

A: Yes.

Q: *Has she ever answered?*

A: No.

Q: *Do you have any pictures of her?*

A: No.

Q: *Did she cry when you left?*

A: Yes. Yes.

Q: *Did you cry when you left?*

A: Yes.

Q: *This was seven years ago?*

A: Yes.

Q: *Have you ever had a girlfriend since then?*

A: No.

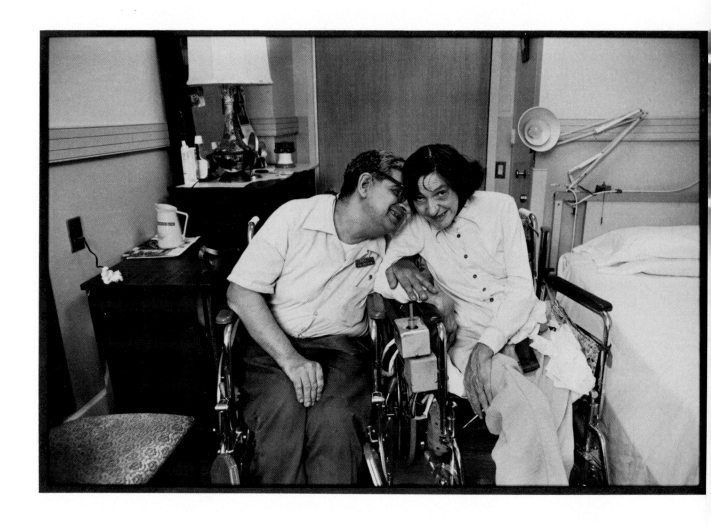

KAY

He means the whole world to me.

SOL

I'm Jewish and she's Catholic, but we don't care about that. We adore each other very much. When we don't see each other even for a couple hours, or overnight, I can't stand it. I can't wait until the next day.

LOIS

The most difficult part [of being in a relationship] is when two people get to feeling real close to each other, and then—all of a sudden—it's no longer there. . . . For me, I think I learned a lot being in a relationship. Now I'm being by myself. . . . I'm happy no one's pursuing me right now, but sad. . . . I don't think it's good to be alone *all* the time. You need people, too. But you need your freedom, also. That pretty much sums it up, I think.

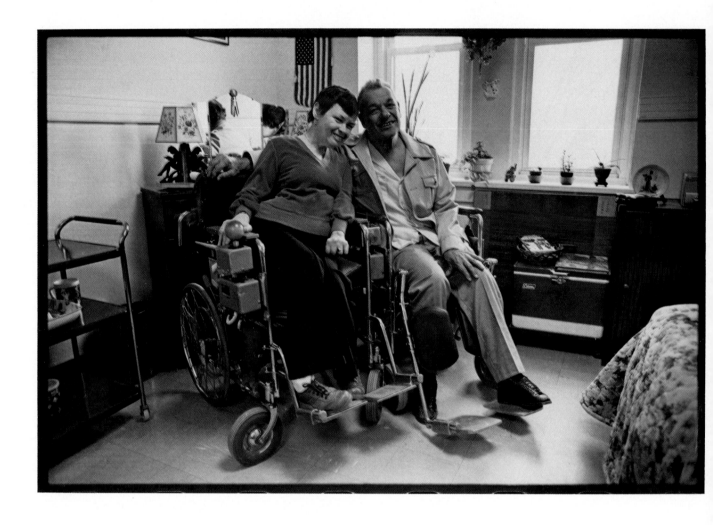

ELEANOR

He means my whole life right now—he does—well, it *is* a strong statement, I know, and to say it in front of him! But I'd really be lost without him right now. . . . I depend on him for so many things. . . . It's been true for thirty-three years.

CARL

I came to Inglis House the year that she was born—nineteen twenty-three. I was nine years old. [Eleanor came in 1948.] We're very compatible. . . . We like the same sports, we like to go to the same kind of movies. . . . We've discussed each other's lives from beginning to end, so we more or less know how each other feels about life and what we expect, and what we don't expect. . . .

EPILOGUE

TONY

Tony, one year after leaving Inglis House,
shown here in his apartment in central Pennsylvania where he now lives with his brother.

BARBARA

Barbara, a few days after the birth of her son. (The baby has been placed with foster parents who bring him regularly to Inglis House to visit her.)

Bob's gravesite in New Jersey. (His wife, Jane, who had not been able to attend his funeral and burial, asked that the author visit the gravesite and place the photograph and flowers at Bob's headstone.)

ANDY AND CAROL

Andy and Carol, moments after exchanging
marriage vows on the grounds of Inglis House,
June 1983.

ANDREA AND WALLY

Andrea, two years after leaving Inglis House,
shown here with her new husband, Wally, at
their trailer home.

Hugh on his last day at Inglis House, August 31, 1984. (The following day, he moved into student housing at a major Eastern university where he is currently completing his studies toward a bachelor's degree.)

AFTERWORD, by Joseph W. Schneider

I am a sociologist who has done research on people's experience of illness and disability. I have thought a good deal about what it means to be disabled in an able-bodied world, but I myself am not physically disabled. I have written this afterword on the premise that looking at Bernard Stehle's photographs of the "incurably romantic" people at Inglis House can be disturbing, both because of questions it raises about these people's lives there and because of the questions it raises about ourselves, what we think of and how we act toward people with disabilities. I try here to anticipate some of these questions and reactions and use them to bridge, in a limited way, the experiences of looking at and reading this book and the experiences of those people in it. To the extent this bridge is begun, readers might spend more time with these images, see more in them, behind them, and in front of them than they would otherwise.

We live in a culture that places a high premium on how people look. A conventional-appearing body is prima facie evidence of "normality." It is of course even better to be considered "beautiful" or "handsome," the recipients of such appraisals in our society becoming personal models or ideals. In this way, body and self are merged, such that physical beauty is thought to tell us something about what kind of person one is. This is similarly true at the other end of the spectrum of physical body-image. Those considered "unattractive" and physically "abnormal" become, by extension, less personally worthy. Disabled people are devalued as persons and become objects of reactions that isolate and segregate them from a variety of social settings. In important ways, such people are in the society but not completely of it. People with disabilities are thus stigmatized, as Erving Goffman has made so clear, just as those with enhanced physical qualities and function are idealized. That we routinely do make these connections is evidenced by the note we make when we encounter beautiful people who fall below our expectations of them as persons, and unattractive people who turn out to be beautiful.

This devaluation is a pervasive element of disabled people's reality. It comes to them not only directly, from others' actions, but also subtly, through their own socialization into our culture, and even at their own hands. Irving Kenneth Zola—himself a person with a physical disability—has noted this process among disabled people, describing how those who have less disabling conditions are ranked higher than those with more severe disabilities. People with disabling mental conditions are at the lowest step of all. Sometimes, those who have certain physically handicapping conditions—such as cerebral palsy—are also assumed to be mentally retarded, thus moving them to an even lower status than they would otherwise occupy in this class system of disability.

The people we see in Stehle's photographs are physically, not mentally, disabled, but they probably have learned to be skeptical of their worth and value as persons. They—indeed, we all—are surrounded by cultural messages that not only is a beautiful body somehow connected to a beautiful person, but more to the point here, that the notions of love, romance, and sexuality are the province of normal and preferably beautiful bodies and people. Couples in love are conventionally described as "radiant," "lovely," "young," "healthy," and expected to be whole. These are appealing, even romantic, notions, and only when we look more closely at the lives of real people do we notice the discrepancy between reality and these cultural images.

Such meanings contribute to a sense that love—being a lover and loved—is incongruous with physical (and surely mental) disabilities. This culturally unlikely combination surely must be why Stehle was moved to make these photographs. He tells us how surprised he was to find romance in such a place as Inglis House. We tend to see people we cannot locate in our conventional categories of body and appearance as asexual, as surely not romantic or lovers. Marcia Millman has made this same point in her study of fat people, where she found that obese people, and obese women in particular, are seen either as asexual or sexually insatiable. One wonders if such definitions are applied to physically handicapped people. Does the idea of an explicit *sexual* relationship between a paralyzed man in a wheelchair and a woman with spinal cord injury seem abnormal, shocking, perhaps disgusting?

When we encounter people, and probably photographs of people, with unmistakably out-of-the-ordinary physical or bodily features, a paradoxical process begins. First, we silently concentrate our attention on those features, reducing the person to them. Virtually all else recedes. They become "that woman with one leg," or "the poor blind girl," or "the man in the wheelchair." We have trouble getting beyond the immediately visible feature as the person's essence—indeed, as the person.

This mirrors the way other devalued minority and "deviant" people are thus reduced. Given this, Stehle's decision to make photographs of *these* people seems almost perverse, as if to highlight precisely that which not only sets them apart but is the very object of devaluation and reduction. How can we ever *see* these people as normal if we have to *look* at them?

A common reaction, then, to Stehle's photographs might be to turn away, either literally, by closing the book or leafing through it hurriedly, or more subtly, by selecting for attention those features of the people and their love stories that are familiar to us, that is, "normal." If we can avoid looking at the twisted hand or face in the photograph, the shriveled leg or wheelchair, and skip over the few explicit references to handicap in the interview excerpts, we can create the comfortable conclusion that these people are, after all, "not so different." It's "the smile," the "twinkle in the eye," the "fierce determination," the "pretty face" that we use to create something familiar to respond to. This is a particularly seductive conclusion in so far as it is true. More to the point, however, it is importantly incomplete.

This normalizing reaction to Stehle's photographs is probably heightened by their theme: the romantic relationships involving people at Inglis House. Being in love certainly is part of the human condition, if not in everyone's experience then in imagination. Well-known conventions of romantic love displayed in these images allow us to see the relationships and those who have them as involving something we can understand and share: arms entwined, sweet smiles, kisses and touches exchanged, endearing words, names, and glances. Sincere affection is expressed, and less happily, the almost palpable fear of rejection and desertion—the experience of a broken heart—is shown. Romantic clichés, indeed. With a sense of relief and proud tolerance, we ourselves can turn to clichés. "Ah, love makes the world go 'round; love conquers all." We add, however, perhaps *soto voce*, the crucial addendum, "*in spite of everything*, including a body like that!"

But this denies both too much of these people's lives and our own to serve any of us well. It implies that these relationships and people are, for all practical purposes, the same as they would be were their bodies in full working order. We must not allow ourselves to ignore where these people live, and why. Their routine experience is hardly "in spite of" their bodies and circumstances. Perhaps *we* can ignore these things. They surely cannot. How do we respond?

Several years ago, Fred Davis interviewed physically handicapped people about their encounters with able-bodied acquaintances. His respondents described the interaction as artificial, stilted, and uncomfortable. In a few instances, however, something very important occurred that transformed the relationship into a free, easy, ostensibly authentic exchange. Davis used one person's own words and called this "breaking through." What was broken through was the mutual pretense that everything was regular, usual, conventional, when it *clearly* was not. Moreover, the "it" was not merely a feature of the larger physical setting, but rather of a person—of that person's *body* and, by extension, his or her self. To deny the disabled piece of that person was, in effect, to deny the person's reality.

The key to this change was that the "normals" were able to accept the particular physical disability before them. They could look at and even talk about the leg, arm, prosthesis, disfigurement as part of the other's *physical* presence. It was, paradoxically, only by taking into account this physical part that interaction and relationships—indeed, this person—could become "normal." When others worked very hard *not* to notice the disabling feature, it overwhelmed the relationship.

In an important sense, Stehle's photographs allow us to *practice* "breaking through" without having actually to risk embarrassing failure, or do the harder work such acceptance in fact involves. We can look, stare, examine the unfamiliar-looking hand, the brace, the shape of the back, with no danger of being caught looking. We can even rehearse what we might say to let the person know we are not denying their reality, listening to our words and altering them to express just what we mean. We might even ask questions about the disability, if that feels right. Alone with these photographs, we can begin to accept the reality that these bodies are not normal, that they require considerable and regular attention and hard work to fit into many routine, mundane activities. These bodies or their parts obviously make it difficult to participate in and even preclude some conventional activities, and in some cases they defy using familiar cultural formulas to manage life's events.

In this process of breaking through, the bodily abnormality gradually recedes for us. As it does, we begin to see *other* things about these people. Their experiences, ways of feeling, expressions, fears and anxieties, hopes and dreams are ones, mostly likely, we have felt and dreamed. In this kind of seemingly contradictory conclusion, that the people and relationships here are *both* normal and not, we begin to appreciate more fully their actual experience. They and their romances are, to be sure, familiar. But they also are quite unfamiliar, particularly in so far as their bodies make a great variety of things considerably more complicated, not only for them but also for their friends and lovers. By imagining the very specific details of their routine activities we can begin to understand more completely how they live and feel.

Beyond dealing with physical competence, the people we see here may have had to struggle even to see themselves as someone attractive or lovable—as the object of desire and as one who can feel and reciprocate it. Perhaps the love story we see is the *first* or one of very few such relationships ever experienced. So these romances—or at least many of them—most probably do become more precious, more overwhelming in their import, than many other "normal" love stories. Such love and affection received and returned become a profound affirmation of the person's essential normality—*as he or she is*, not "in spite of" it. Such affirmations of self are, of course, just as significant for those whose bodies seem to be normal, and do not always come easily or without significant costs. The difference may be that we come to take our bodies for granted as objects others could love and desire. We, most likely, have to work less hard to realize such experiences than those who are physically disabled. What a joy it must be indeed for these people to give the lie to such superficial but oppressive cultural lessons.

By hurrying to see them as "normal after all," we deny a significant part of their reality and of them. We must see that bodies and selves, although certainly linked, are not the same; that while bodies may enable or thwart certain aspects of self, self typically transcends, is more than, body. This is not to say that they are independent of one another. By forcing us to look and, I hope, see, Stehle's photographs can lead us to think seriously about both our connections to and separations from people with disabilities, as well as about how our own bodies and selves are inseparable yet not determinatively linked. By focusing our attention on these normal people's bodies, these photographs allow us to see beyond such physical disabilities, but they do not allow us to deny them, something that in fact may be more easy to do in face-to-face encounters.

Beyond *our* reactions to the people and relationships displayed here, other important questions turn on the place of Inglis House in their lives and stories. In thinking so much about breaking through, it is possible almost to forget that these people live in what Goffman called a "total institution," a formal, bureaucratic organization that controls, standardizes, and schedules virtually all aspects of patients', inmates', prisoners', or residents' lives. Sociological studies of such institutions document the tension inherent in such places between individuality, privacy, and self, on the one hand, and imposed rules and regulations, sameness, predictability, and public surveillance, on the other. Residents of such institutions must regularly work to retain a sense of their individuality.

We do not see much of the common areas of Inglis House in these photographs, but we can see that residents' rooms, shown often, display ample evidence of these efforts, of what Jaber Gubrium has called "furniture of self." This furniture consists of material objects—photographs, posters, figurines, momentos from times and circumstances gone by, actual pieces of favorite or meaningful furniture that personalize space and make it their own, make it home. For those who live at Inglis House, the institution may be their house, but their rooms are their homes. They are likely the only places in the institution where residents can freely display and express themselves.

The relationships Stehle shows us certainly must rely on the sanctity of this personal space. Given the nature of such institutions, one wonders how staff at Inglis House regard these and other couples? Do the relationships described have staff blessings or are they considered troublesome to institutional routine? Are they seen as possible grounds for criticism from people and agencies outside the institution, such as members of residents' families or watchdog organizations? How far do staff allow these relationships to go? These questions bring us back to residents' rooms as inviolable space—"our shrine," as one woman called it—and make us wonder how staff and institutional policy deal with resident sexual activity. I speculated, for instance, about whether closed doors in Inglis House insure privacy, whether a couple pictured near a bed would be allowed to be *in* it, together, doing sexual things. Even if this is permitted, how do some of these lovers handle not being able to get into bed and/or have sex without the assistance of a third person? A question that only has begun to be asked by many institution officials is whether and how staff should educate, instruct, and support residents in experiencing sexual pleasure and fulfillment when they are unable to use standard cultural recipes.

This raises again the problem of the impoverished culture disabled people face around questions of love, romance, and sex. What they learned about love and sex—what they are and how to *do* them—was taken from the conventional culture. Such meanings and guides often may seem not to work, given their circumstances. There are, for instance, few readily available discussions of how to attain sexual fulfillment when one's body will not cooperate to fit standard routines. To the extent these people pursue and experience themselves as lovers and sexual people, they—perhaps with those who support them—must create culture to solve their routine problems of living, including being sexual in a community of physically disabled people.

What about contraception? Pregnancy? Parenthood? What happened to the woman who became a new mother while at Inglis House? How do staff regard love between people of the same gender? We read a poignant remark by one man that suggests the subject is very much closeted and taboo there and, one suspects, in most places like it. Such questions about sexual expression are just under the surface of these images. They touch the larger issues of autonomy and personhood in institutions, and allow us a glimpse at a darker side of this community's life that Stehle does not and perhaps could not show.

Several residents are shown with or talk about mates or friends who live outside Inglis House and who are less disabled than the person inside or not disabled at all. We know little of how these relationships might be different from those between residents, how the lovers manage to bring and keep their lives together, against a variety of physical, social, and psychological odds. A few people speak about these problems, but it is difficult to gain much insight into how institutionalization affects relationships already established before one person enters, relationships that somehow begin after people enter, relationships between residents when both are inside and, later, when one person leaves Inglis House and the other remains.

Can places such as Inglis House be humanized to support and encourage the kind of cultural work needed to create viable solutions to severely disabled people's problems? It is another paradox, although sweeter than some, that perhaps by coming to Inglis House, people with physical disabilities could be empowered to gain more rather than experience less control over their lives. After all, many of the romances Stehle shows us would not have occurred without the institution. Although we are not told, the residents came together to press for a change in the institution's name, from the starkly grim "home for incurables" to "home for physically disabled persons." Is it possible that from such a "total institution" could come new ways of thinking, acting, and relating that might enable its residents, by *drawing on* their disabilities, to become even *more* normal than they are? This seems to be precisely what other physically handicapped people, along with former mental patients, and various other devalued groups, are doing in our public life. It is an exciting, hopeful possibility.

Finally, to end with a corrective for perhaps too much optimism, we might wonder about those people at Inglis House Stehle does not show us, either because they chose not to be photographed or give permission for their photographs to be used, or because they were not involved in such important relationships. While we can be happy at any instances of human sharing and fulfillment in places like Inglis House, what of those people beyond the eye of the camera, out of view? Who else lives there and in other facilities like it? Who are their friends? Who cares for them? Talks? Listens? Touches? We need more insights such as those offered by Stehle's photographs to avoid an overly romantic view and to help us appreciate how our fellow men and women, afflicted by both physical and mental disabilities, spend their days, months, years, and lives, quite shut away from our view and concern.